Contents

Praise For 'Voice Of A Woman Leader' xi

Foreword xiv

About The Author xvi

Admiration For Author Spoorti Nayak xix

Introduction xxi

Chapter 1: Women Empowerment Starts With You 1

- Enhance her Self-Esteem 2
- Promote positivity shutdown negativity 3
- Exhibit your honest self 3
- Be a mentor for female colleague 4
- Lead by example 5
- Empower newly working mothers 6
- Pandemic; A boon for Corporate women 7

Chapter 2: Challenges Of Working Women And How To Overcome Them 9

- Stagnant growth in career 10
- Office Politics 10
- Unrecognized Efforts at Workplace 12
- Biased Pay scale 13
- Delayed Promotion 14
- Lessened Opportunities 14
- Constant Failures 15
- Fear of losing the current job 16

- Distorted Work-life balance 17
- Existence of Male Ego. 18
- Safety and Dignity 19
- No ownership on her own earning. 20
- Sexual Harassment 21

Chapter 3: How To Climb Up Corporate Ladder, Faster 23

- Make a Plan 24
- Keep Networking 25
- Work Hard and Work Smart 26
- Dream Beyond the Job Description 27
- Be an asset to the company 28
- Think and act a level above 30
- Be a team player 31

Chapter 4: Powerful Body Language – Courage To Act And Dare To Lead 33

- Right Facial expression 34
- Power of 'Power Poses'. 35
- Indulge in Active Listening 36
- Firm Handshakes 37
- Talk with your hands 38
- Look out for Vocal Pitch 39
- Effective communication 39
- Emotional Intelligence 40
- Avoid Fidgeting. 40
- Things to avoid while stressing on Body language 41

Dedicating this book to my beloved

*Mom **Ms. SEEMA NAYAK** and Dad **Mr. B.V NAYAK***

VOICE OF A WOMAN
LEADER

*How to
Lead with
Integrity,
Insight and
Inclusiveness*

SPOORTI NAYAK

BlueRose ONE .com
Stories Matter
NewDelhi • London

BLUEROSE PUBLISHERS
India | U.K.

For permissions requests or inquiries regarding this publication, please contact:

BLUEROSE PUBLISHERS
www.BlueRoseONE.com
info@bluerosepublishers.com
+91 8882 898 898
+4407342408967

ISBN: 978-93-5819-530-9

Cover Design: Muskan Sachdeva
Typesetting: Pooja Sharma

First Edition: January 2024

Chapter 5: 8 Leadership Styles – How To Find Your Own Style...43

- Autocratic Leadership...44
- Pacesetting Leadership..45
- Transformational Leadership 46
- Coaching Leadership...47
- Democratic Leadership..48
- Affiliative Leadership..49
- Delegative Leadership 50
- Servant Leadership 51
- Why is it important to know your leadership style?...........52

Chapter 6: Process Of Women Being Stronger Leaders In Workplace...54

- Fight for Mindset of Equality as Reality 55
- Women embracing their Natural Leadership style 56
- Engage in Honest Open Communication. 56
- Grow connections with your team 57
- Vitalize Professional and Personal Growth. 58
- Maintain Optimistic Attitude 60
- Mentor employees instead of dumping orders 60
- Set Clear Employee goals and Expectations. 61
- Handout Feedbacks on Employee Performances............62
- Ask for your Feedback as a Leader.............................63
- New Ideas are Lifelines: *Be Open to Them* 63
- Recognize your own motivation..................................64

Chapter 7: How To Boost Employee Engagement – Make Work Environment Fun...66

- Allocate Time for Fun...67
- Offer Unique Employee discounts. 68
- Vitalize Open Communication. 68
- Use Value-based Employee Recognition 69
- Know your employees 69
- Create Opportunities for Collaboration 70
- Elucidate on Employee Contribution 70
- Prioritize work-life balance...71
- Offer Role Flexibility 72
- Maintain Transparency 73
- Offer wellness and growth opportunities.........................73
- Offer Coaching and Mentoring.......................................74
- Provide multiple options for Feedback 74
- Make a point to integrate new hires...............................75
- Develop a strong Company culture 75
- Support Employee goals..76
- Act On Feedbacks 77
- Celebrate Milestones 77

Chapter 8: Learn How To Adapt Remote And Hybrid Working In Organizations 78

- Work From Home; An easy answer to Increased Productivity 79
- Improved Work-life balance; The best outcome of Remote Working – 80
- Eliminating Commute; Notable Benefit of opting Remote work 81

- Fosters Healthy lifestyle; Best benefit of adapting to Remote work 82
- Evolution of Remote Working 83
- Current State of Remote Working 84
- Hybrid Working Model: *An Emerging Solution* 85
- Future and Remote Working 86

Chapter 9: How To Improve Your Work-Life Balance - Challenging But Crucial 87

- Accept that there is no perfect work-life balance 88
- Find a Job that interests you 89
- Prioritize your health 89
- Don't fear unplugging 90
- Take Vacations 91
- Allocate time for yourself and your close ones 92
- Set Boundaries and work hours 93
- Learn to Set Goal and Prioritize 93
- Support the idea of 'Being a Supportive Manager' 94
- Know the craving of your Employees 95
- Set a Good example 95
- Educate employees about their options 95

Chapter 10: Life Is Too Short To Not Love What You Do For A Living 97

- Feeling Fulfilled – *The best feeling your job can offer* 98
- Being Passionately Productive 99
- Inspiring Others 100
- Success Follows – *when you do what you love* 100
- What did you want to be as a Child? 101

- What would your Family/Friends Identify as your Strengths? 102

- Who was your biggest role model growing up?.................... 103

- What did you truly dislike doing?.. 103

Special Heartfelt Thanks 105

Connect With Author 106

Praises For 'Voice Of A Woman Leader'

My hearty congratulations to Spoorti for picking up such a relevant topic and assembling the most important tips and pointers for all women trying to build their career one step at a time. Must read for every career-oriented woman. This book will give dozens of inspirations and sparkle ambition. All the topics in the book are so relevant in the current times and can act as a step-by-step plan for carving careers.

Surabhi Dewra, Chief Executive Officer (CEO) of Career Guide, TOP 50 Global Edutech Leaders, Best Women Leaders in India 40 Under 40, Fame India 25 Powerful Women.

***

I am privileged to share my thoughts on the easy-read book "Voice of a women leader."

Every chapter describes the step-by-step approach towards" how to lead with integrity, insight, and inclusiveness. "It has something different to offer for readers and budding women leaders. She stresses women's latent strength and compassion and makes you believe that you can lead from the front and be ideal for someone to follow.

Her easily readable writing style and the steps suggested make it easier for you to implement each of the suggestions in your leadership style.

I liked chapter 4 on Body language - the courage to act and dare to lead; the steps suggested, though they sound common sense, easily implementable, and very apt for budding leaders. For example: providing a firm handshake makes a lot of difference in communicating your confidence and competency.

I highly recommend this to every women leader; one can see and relate that many things in their approach are lacking, and they derive courage from them.

I am glad to see a unique effort by this young author to contribute back to the Women Leaders community; indeed, it is a commendable effort by Spoorti. I wish her the best.

Manjanath Nayak, Global Chief Delivery Officer (CDO)
MICROLAND, USA

***

Spoorti has put in a lot of effort, dedication and courage in penning her thoughts and experience into this book. She describes the hurdles of working women in the professional world, and offers practical solutions based on her experience on how to overcome challenges. I find Spoorti's analysis of different leadership styles very insightful and relevant.

I have personally worked with many coworkers, who have shown courage to face adversities and challenges as they come and inspire everyone in the way they dealt with situations, turning adversities into positive outcomes. The anecdotes that Spoorti has shared in the book resonate very well with these challenges, and the solutions she provides to rise above them is exemplary and achievable. In short, this book talks about motivation, leveraging your strengths and determination to achieve heights in the corporate world, despite difficulties.

I thoroughly enjoyed reading the book and strongly recommended it to all aspiring to become successful leaders in their field of work.

Ramakrishna Alapati, Chief Operating Officer (COO)
at Ephanti Inc.

***

Spoorti is a unique technology and change leader with versatility and breadth. Spoorti brings all of her insight and experience into Voice Of A Woman Leader, a must read book that professionals can use to get the most out of their talent. With her ideas and solutions Spoorti will has defined leadership paradigm for the years to come. Her book will help all readers, men and women, to become better and more effective leaders. It is an absolutely valuable book to help us build the lives we want to lead and world we want to live in. The strategies and techniques discussed in the book are simple to understand, easy to apply and are very effective in enabling you to achieve the career outcomes that you desire.

Madhavi Chippada, Assistant Vice President (AVP)
Bank of America India Pvt Ltd.

Foreword by

Mrs. Lakshmi Hebbalkar

Minister of Women and Child Development, Disabled and
Senior Citizens Empowerment in the Government of Karnataka

***

The history speaks for itself as we see women leading up ahead equally with men whilst making quintessential decisions of a company, or managing a whole lot of things perfectly. Voice of a woman leader was always meant to be heard the right way. I guess this marvelous book is an example of how empathetic, knowledgeable, and thoughtful the impact can be on the society.

This book 'VOICE OF A WOMAN LEADER' is a marvelous book penned down to speak for those who are determined to look through the problems arising in corporate life and solve them. It serves as the solution to all aspiring young minds who wish to achieve noticeable success and growth on the corporate ladder.

The main focus this book drives is about the challenges faced by women whilst working and having a personal life, what are the ways to climb up the success ladder faster, how powerful one's body language can be, how to implement the best possible working model and more.

Being a political leader and someone with a zeal to assert and imbibe stability and certainty, I have come a long way facing the difficulties along with my supporters and slashing the patriarchy and wanting to do, what I do better has been my goal for a long time now. This book is an absolute honor to Spoorti Nayak for doing a great job and bringing out this valuable piece which is a one-stop solution for all your corporate problems.

It was very recently before the 2023 Karnataka assembly election results came out, I felt how much necessitated we all are to have a woman leading a state/country/constituencies. Books like these inspire thousands of aspiring leaders to come out and do something profound.

Spoorti has nailed leadership strategies for corporate professionals in this book. I found this book to be very practical and full of advices which can be easily applied in the workplace to turn around your career and life.

This book provokes one to think, to bring the actions in tune with one's value system. The author has given facts and figures interspersed with real life experiences, which makes it even more special. This impresses upon us the need for a change in attitude. My heartfelt wishes to Spoorti for writing an impactful book that will benefit our society.

Must Read, Inspire and Lead!

All the best to Spoorti.

Lakshmi Hebbalkar held the position of general secretary of the Karnataka Pradesh Mahila Congress Committee for a brief period before being asked to head the Belagavi District Congress Committee in 2010 as its first woman president. She was reelected to the assembly in 2023 and was appointed the Minister of Women and Child Development as part of the Siddaramaiah ministry.

About The Author

Spoorti Nayak is a Director for Program and Project management at LTIMindtree and she is a Project management professional from IIM Kozhikode with 15 years of project management success. Spoorti's agile and project management experience along with her coaching and training abilities gives her the perspective needed to guide teams and leaders. She knows the transformation path is rocky, yet possible. She started her career as a Software engineer and evolved into senior roles like Project manager, Agile transformation coach, Program leader and Director of Project Management. Her IT experiences span multiple industry domains like Healthcare, Banking and Financial Services.

Spoorti is a mother of two and is fortunate that prior to LTIMindtree, she served multiple global corporates like Bank of America, Vsoft, ADP, and United Health Group (Optum Global Solutions) with different minds and different work cultures around the world. She has been with these global corporates for more than a decade. She helped them to do better than what they were doing yesterday. As a leader and people manager, she always helped others to rebuild careers by offering encouragement, and guidance also helped to accelerate career growth and make successful career transitions.

When Spoorti had her second child, she came under immense pressure to quit her job. She constantly had her peer working women telling her that managing a home and career was not something expected out of women. She was scared to step aside as it would reflect on all women. She took up the challenge to show that it was possible. So with the same spirit, she is hoping to help women who would like to build their careers in the corporate world.

Spoorti has been grateful for having the complete support from her husband, family and kids. She believes that they're an integral part of growing up the corporate ladder. Without them, she wouldn't have been what she is today. She owes it to her parents, and supportive husband.

"I hope career-driven women will not give up easily on their dreams and aspirations. They are strong-willed and determined to achieve whatever they want. This not only helps them professionally but also improves their personal lives significantly. Instead of fearing sitting at home, embrace and adopt the change openly." – **Spoorti Nayak**.

Spoorti says, "Speaking of working in one of her organisation, our workforce is young and we have some mothers who would not come to work because they were breastfeeding their babies and had young kids. These women needed additional facilities at work to feel comfortable. So I met a group of women and came up with ideas on how to make the workplace more diverse. This led to many wonderful ideas providing work from home, extended maternity leaves, encouraging a Hybrid work model and reducing the number of hours at the office and regularizing/extending work hours. So it decreases stress and increases the productivity of working women. And also bringing these concerns to the notice of human resources so that organisations can make more flexible and inclusive work policies for working mothers. I never thought I would write a book. I am not a journalist or sociologist, but I decided to speak out after talking to many numbers of women, listening to their struggles and sharing my own, while realizing that the gains we made are not enough and may even be slipping."

"I dedicate this book to any woman who wants to increase her chances of making it to the top of her career and pursue any goal she dreams about. This includes women at all stages of their lives and careers, from those who are just starting out to those who are taking a break and may want to jump back in. I am also writing this for any man who wants to understand what a woman- a colleague, wife, mother, or daughter, is up against so that he can do his part to build an equal world", quotes the author.

Being a remarkable leader, she has instilled confidence in the team as well as contributed to the growth of the department /clients through improved team productivity and excellent delivery on time. As a leader she has always provided focus and drives the team forward. She empowers team members to work to their full potential, by taking full responsibility for the decision making. She believes that the role of a leader is not to come up with all the great ideas, in fact to simply create an environment in which great ideas find space to bloom. She has given opportunities to all junior and senior team members to come up with their thoughts and innovations to build an effective solution.

With effective management skills, Spoorti has incorporated agile culture in the team. She has shown that "team" is not just people who work at the same time in the same place. A real team is a group of very different individuals who enjoy working together and who share a commitment to working cohesively to help the organization achieve their common goals and fulfill its purposes.

As a recognition to her strong leadership skills, project management, delivery acumen, team and client management by instilling positive impact, she has received several awards and recognitions from the organizations she served.

Spoorti holds multiple certifications like Project Management Professional (PMP), Agile Certified Coach(ICP-ACC), SAFe-Agilist, Kanban Management Professional (KMP), and Certified Scrum Master (CSM).

She has completed her Bachelor of Engineering in Computer Science from VTU, Karnataka and is a Certified Professional in Project management from IIM Kozhikode (EPGPC).

Admiration For Author Spoorti Nayak

The remarkable achievements and inspiring journey of a woman leader who has penned a maiden book "VOICE OF A WOMAN LEADER", left an indelible mark on the corporate world. Spoorti Nayak, a name that resonates with success, empowerment, and change. Spoorti's life and accomplishments are a testament to her remarkable upbringing, passion, and dedication to making a difference.

Spoorti Nayak hails from a nurturing and supportive family background that instilled in her the values of resilience, determination, and the belief that anything is possible. Growing up, she was encouraged to pursue her dreams and excel in her chosen field. These early experiences provided her with a strong foundation and nurtured her leadership spirit.

As a Project Management Professional from IIM Kozhikode, one of India's premier management institutes, Spoorti was equipped with the knowledge and skills to navigate the complex business world. With 15 years of experience under her belt, she emerged as a force to be reckoned with. Her expertise and insights in the corporate realm have made her a respected authority in her field.

Spoorti's journey took a significant turn when she penned her book, "VOICE OF A WOMAN LEADER", This powerful literary creation is organized into ten chapters, each addressing critical aspects of women's empowerment in the workplace. The book delves into topics such as improving working conditions for women, the challenges they face, and effective strategies to overcome these hurdles. It also provides guidance on climbing the corporate ladder faster and emphasizes the importance of adopting suitable work environments.

One of the central themes of Spoorti's book is the pursuit of gender equality in the workplace. She sheds light on the need for organizations to create an inclusive environment that nurtures the talents and aspirations of both men and women. By exploring the power of body language, Spoorti demonstrates how women can harness their strengths to communicate effectively and assert their leadership in any setting.

Moreover, "VOICE OF A WOMAN LEADER", goes beyond professional growth and touches upon the significance of maintaining a healthy mind and body. Spoorti emphasizes the importance of practices like yoga and routine exercises to enhance overall well-being. She understands that for individuals to thrive, they must be mentally and physically fit.

Another crucial aspect discussed in Spoorti's book is the importance of leadership styles and employee engagement. She provides valuable insights on how leaders can boost employee morale and create an environment that fosters growth and innovation. Additionally, Spoorti stresses the significance of work-life balance, recognizing that it is essential for individuals to find harmony between their personal and professional lives.

Spoorti Nayak's book, "VOICE OF A WOMAN LEADER", stands as a beacon of inspiration for all women and men aspiring to make their mark in the corporate world. Her words of wisdom, gleaned from years of experience and expertise, offer practical guidance for overcoming challenges and excelling in any industry. Through her book, Spoorti empowers women to be leaders, to embrace their unique strengths, and to create workplaces where equality prevails.

In conclusion, Spoorti Nayak's journey as a successful woman leader and author embodies the spirit of determination, resilience, and empowerment. Her book, "VOICE OF A WOMAN LEADER", provides a roadmap for all working professionals to navigate the challenges of the corporate world, embrace their authentic selves, and make a lasting impact. Let us celebrate Spoorti Nayak's achievements and draw inspiration from her remarkable story. May her example continue to ignite the flames of change and empower countless women to pursue their dreams fearlessly.

G B Chebbi, IPS Karnataka India

Introduction

A leader is someone who realizes the worth of team growth and inclusiveness of every small member of the team. Integrity and Insight play along together in the making of an effective leader. Being a remarkable leader can instill confidence in the team as well as contribute to the growth of the department through improved team productivity.

Being a leader, and developing the leadership qualities can be achieved only in a longer run. While, trying to be there can be the extraordinary start. Instances that come up in an employee's daily life can be equally stressing and productive at the same time. A leader will always provide focus and drives the team forward. She/He will empower team members to work at their full potential, by taking full responsibility for the decision making.

Why this book is important?

This book serves as a one-stop solution for all your corporate juggles and makes you feel like success is not a far-fetched fruit, but instead is a long-term hard-worked fruit, which is likely achievable. This book has been written with utmost hope that it will eventually instill a sense of peace and establishing powerful workplace environment. Having leaders to constantly guide and lead a team through, has not been anything less than a blessing. Reading this book will make an employee/leader pen down their entire success ideology for the future.

It merely acts as a silent motivator and provides tons of self-confidence and as a bridge to inclusive growth.

Who can relate to this book?

Anybody who has been self-doubting their capabilities, someone who has been dreaming of leading and integrating a strong team at corporate levels, people working in an environment where growth matters, all of them can relate to the book.. There's a lot this book has in store to offer. From the ground-level employees to the top level executives, this book is going to be your friend at all stages. Considering the author bags varieties of experiences in corporate world, this book is realistic and addresses every small detail of the working force.

By the end of this book, you will have a clear picture of how to deal with corporate plights and how to handle your stressful work, of any sort. This is a modernized problem, which needed a modern approach towards solution. 'VOICE OF A WOMAN LEADER' has always been something that's gone heard yet unheard. It's time to take a step back, understand the problems and find solutions in a profound way.

CHAPTER 1

Women Empowerment Starts With You

Life had been a roller coaster ride for me, during my second pregnancy. The postpartum phase has taught me one of the biggest lessons of life. The struggles I faced being a working mother pushed me into taking up the initiative and stance of penning down the effective problems faced by a woman in corporate universe. That's when I realized how many voices went unheard and unsound.

Wanting to take up an initiative and actually initiating it are two different things.

Although Women Empowerment has been one of the constantly recurring topics in debate and group discussions during hiring processes among students, the implementation, progress and adaptation still remain almost unnoticeable.

Centuries-long fight for the equal rights of women has led to the current developed state of social, economic and political ethereal lives. Women empowerment just doesn't happen over the years on its own, it needs attention to detail, relevant actions, and an exhaustive hunt for solutions.

What's more? Women are more likely to get "glass cliff" positions — leadership opportunities that are high stakes, precarious, and have a high likelihood of failure. Given this, it's not surprising that many women said that the single most important thing organizations could do to attract and retain talented women is to admonish sexism and offer gender parity in pay, experiences, and opportunities for success.

Empowering women is essential to the health and social development of families, communities and countries. When women are living safe, fulfilled and productive lives, they can reach their full potential.

Women Want a Calling — Not Just a 9-to-5. Many women talked about having personally meaningful work that connects to their values, purpose, and work-life balance. These reasons describe a specific type of employment that social scientists call "a calling." Callings are jobs that people feel drawn to pursue; find intrinsically enjoyable and meaningful, and see as a central part of their identity. Research shows that experiencing work as a "calling" is related to increased job satisfaction.

The unpopularly popular quote says that "Behind every successful man, there is a woman". Why Behind? Why not besides? A strong woman will lead a troop full of workers ahead with respect, honour, success and integrity.

Leader – A person who helps the environment around her/him grow along with them.

Let's talk about how 'YOU' can play a part in empowering women –

- **Enhance her Self-Esteem** – A woman is a key to untapping the potential of other women. There's nothing more attractive to see the women around you grow and be confident in their own skin because of the motivation and inspiration you've set. Teach her to set boundaries around herself, May it be work or personal life. For what it's worth, she will see herself growing in your shade. Guide her about professional growth whilst satisfying her personal needs.

  Women in India prosper through meaningful work that allows them to balance their domestic responsibilities, with opportunities for social and economic empowerment. Widen the term called 'comfort'. Set examples of women who have lived and achieved mountains full of successes, amidst critical times. Form a whole new definition of 'WOMEN EMPOWERMENT' for her.

  Impart the true sense of Feminism in each one looking up to you. Why do we have to compromise on Family or Work? Why is it just on us? Teach her that a family and an organization is run by more than just one person. Help her awaken her true self. Empower them to become role models and change makers in their families and communities.

- **Promote positivity shutdown negativity** – There is nothing more prosperous than a positive and vibrant work environment. Women are constantly exposed to the realistic world with unrealistic expectations about looks, way of work, IQ, and much more illogical negativity. A great leader will help other women feel safe in a challenging environment. Preach that human potential is boundless and irreplaceable.

  Statistics say, nearly 2.4 Billion Women Globally Don't Have the Same Economic Rights as Men. Negativity from within and around hinders the growth of an individual and an organization.

  Compared with men at the same level, women are doing more to support their teams and advance diversity, equity, and inclusion efforts. They are also more likely to be allies to women of color. This critical work is going unrecognized and unrewarded by most companies, and that has concerning implications. As a leader, be the voice of the voiceless and raise up the issues surfacing, by putting up a legal fight.

  Some steps organizations can take are; Adopting permanent family-friendly policies, flexible scheduling, or supporting different work styles like hybrid or remote will open the doors to extraordinary talent by meeting employees where they are, both in life and location, by shutting down the negativity.

- **Exhibit your honest self** – Women influencers like Sojourner Truth, Catherine the Great, Maya Angelou, Rosa Parks, and Malala Yousafzai, have set an astounding example by telling the true story of their success, coming out of a challenging yet degrading environment. Although it is quite tricky and maybe traumatic to yourself, talking openly about your story might definitely turn useful to tons of women out there.

  A true sense of honesty and openness builds a relationship between you and the ones working for you, unbreakable.

  Start by narrating what kept you from your growth, the hours you put into preparing yourself mentally for failure, when you manifested success, and what pushed you to reach where you are today.

Exhibiting your true self will only bring light to the people who work for you/under you. Nobody said that being a leader is easy. It is very simple to bark out orders and dismiss someone if they are not performing, but it takes work to coach, mentor, inspire and motivate your team o perform their optimum best. That's the fundamental difference between a leader and a manager.

As a leader, create a culture where your people are inspired to create great ideas, and where the dreamers are encouraged to dream big. Constantly inspire your team to perform the best, which ultimately will lift the organizational progress.

I am manifesting an increase in women in leadership and an increase in investment in women-owned and run startups because of a trend we're seeing in the overall tech industry—employees are prioritizing relational factors at work over transactional. A lack of relational factors is the top reason people are citing for quitting: they don't feel valued by their organization, they don't feel valued by their managers, or they don't feel a sense of belonging at work.

- **Be a mentor for female colleague** – Women have suffered long enough with discrimination, racism, casteism, and unrealistic standards of the corporate world. A strong leader is supposed to have their female colleagues' backs when and wherever necessary.

Setting an example like standing up for someone isn't as precarious as it sounds. Learn to stand up for what's right and to shut down what's wrong, may it be bullying or discrimination of any sort.

To become one of the greatest of leaders, you must get comfortable with being very uncomfortable at times to continue your growth toward great leadership because, in many instances, the best things in life are often found outside your comfort zone.

Make sure you bring a fully functioning system into effect that will take up action whenever deemed necessary. This will help develop confidence in you.

A woman if she wills, can create and merge kingdoms, or destroy them to ashes at the same time, history stands stiff as proof.

Studies have recorded that women in South Asia have only two-thirds of their legal rights as compared to men.

"Women cannot achieve equality in the workplace if they are on an unequal footing at home," said Carmen Reinhart, Senior Vice President and Chief Economist of the World Bank Group. Equality is the basic right a woman could ask for at her workplace.

"The role of a leader is not to come up with all the great ideas, the role is to simply create an environment in which great ideas find space to bloom and happen."

Let us also normalize women and minorities in leadership roles and, with this shift, we will also begin to see higher collaboration across industry lines.

- **Lead by example** – If you are the one who's holding a position for which you have struggled and suffered for multiple years, then women below you, look up to you. Carrying the poise and Aura around you, as though you were born and blessed with it. Tell them how long you've fought to be exactly where you are today. Make them believe that you have walked, tripped, stood up and learned on the same road that they're walking on today.

  Women will end up finding solace in you if you impart to them the difficulties they're facing today, which were worse when you walked down the same road. Tell them your stories of sleepless nights, anxious hours, and frustrating days of uncertainty. Project your ups and downs from the past, and then show that your hard work paid off in the end.

  We hesitate, we question ourselves, and we let our lack of confidence hold us back. It's much easier for you to spot the potential in another woman than it is for her to see it in herself. You are the mirror to her.

Make sure that your female coworkers are comfortable sharing something extremely private, like a health issue.

"Great leaders have a genuine interest in others. They have a desire to build a relationship with their team, to know the people working with them, and to encourage everyone on their team to be the best they can be."

- **Empower newly working mothers** – It is never as easy as it looks like for a newly made mom to switch between her personal and professional space. As a leader, there is a lot you can do to help her mentally be strong. The work-life balance has to be earned a hard way for most new mothers. You can stand up for her by offering her help to babysit her infant or ask someone to do it on her behalf. Set up an alternative wherein she can give her best to your organization when she's least distracted by her child's worry.

Offer and fight for longer maternity leaves as compared to the current offerings. Create awareness among your colleagues, about how crucial postpartum is, for a woman. Bid in for her absence and offer shorter working hours for her. Offer flexibility in where, how and when they work. Allowing paid maternity leaves during her last days of pregnancy will work wonders for her.

Paid time off was rated as the most important perk, followed by healthcare benefits, paid leadership development, flexible schedules, and opportunities to move up in the organization. Make them aware of how much they can achieve personally and professionally.

There should be prominence for hiring initiatives on Returnship, especially targeting the return of working mothers, and developing pathways towards leadership for women. Leadership should also be redefined to be inclusive, and to amplify the uniqueness of gender, race, age, and abilities.

"Leadership is not about welding authority or creating an environment of fear; it's all about empowering people and empowering your team to become the very best version of themselves. The common misconception about leadership, is that it means exerting power over the ones below you. Whereas its mostly the mutual growth."

- **Pandemic; A boon for Corporate women** – Although millions of lives were lost during the COVID-19 pandemic in India and all of world, this has proved to be one of the biggest game-changers for women career in the history. Significant shift in the mindsets of people by committing to strengthen their stances on diversity, equity, and inclusion. Throughout this pandemic, our roles and responsibilities have shifted quite a bit; many women put a pause on their professional careers to focus on family and health. It taught us the importance of being valued.

Women started officially taking over bigger roles from an organizational perspective, which proved the hidden fact that there's nothing stopping women from rising to newer heights in corporate field, even amidst global pandemic. In 2022, women will be the change that has been a long time in the making.

I have personally witnessed companies and organizations shifting towards more purpose-driven, people-centered working models, rather than with a competitive mindset between men and women. The way you train the future leaders in midway from changing.

Women especially are emboldened more now than ever (grateful for pandemic) to be the change they wish to see in their own lives and for the world we live in. I believe in the year ahead, we will see more women make the moves from their current roles and careers they've built to take on entrepreneurship and build the companies, products, cultures, teams, and workplaces they want to see in the world and be a part of.

Women leaders from corporate like Karen Lynch, Rosalind Brewer, Gail Boudreaux, and Mary Barra, who have top ranks in Fortune 500 rank in 2021, have set up an example for all of us to look up to. As this moves from an anomaly to an expectation, we will see more investor support for women leaders at all levels in 2022—giving a chance for more voices and styles to build the next generation of companies.

The importance of remote work goes unnoticed yet again. Remote work allows women who are caretakers, coming back from pregnancy or illness, or entering a new field, to thrive in business no matter where they're located. With more women ready to participate in leadership roles, companies will benefit from diverse viewpoints and experiences that will help move their businesses forward.

CHAPTER 2

Challenges Of Working Women And How To Overcome Them

Since ancient times, women have struggled their way out of being considered powerless and incapable of managing work and home altogether. I have known people who talk feminism and act just as opposite to it. True sense of feminism is when you treat and provide women with the similar opportunities, pay and respect at home and workplace. The struggles a woman goes through at workplace is sidelined by most working above their hierarchy. The status and hard work that a woman deserves has to be conveyed with due respect and honor.

In today's world, there is no such profession that doesn't seem suitable for a woman. Women have been subject to long term exploitation at workplace physically, mentally, and sexually. Why is it always expected for a woman to compromise with their careers? When it comes to having a work-life balance?

The exploitations of women are although visible and felt, actions against them to be stopped is far from being taken. Primarily the key to strengthening the social status of a working woman lies in her own hands. Women need to be more assertive and aware of their own rights at home as well as at workplace. Unless woman decides to raise voice against her exploitation, whether at economic, social or sexual level, the goal of women's empowerment cannot be achieved.

I, personally have felt every bit of discrimination and have witnessed loads of such fascism at workplace and thus decided to pen down my perspective of the challenges faced by women and on how to overcome them.

Some of the prominent challenges faced by working women are -

- **Stagnant growth in career** – Although women are told that they are going to be treated equally at workplace, over their contract agreements, it somehow is confined to just the paper and is not functional up to the mark. The growth with respect to career is always comparative to that of opposite gender. The disparity has always surfaced among how the growth graph ranges for a man and a woman, with similar experience and hard work.

  It has seemed that the reason is unknown, but in most workplaces, there's a general feeling that men advance faster, and women are deemed 'incompetent', even when they haven't been given the opportunity to prove themselves. They need to work a little harder and extra in order to earn the reward they deserve, while it's easier for male competent of same institution.

  The growth of a woman in a corporate field can be approximated to be stagnant and comparatively of lower standards compared to that of men. Women working in the same hierarchy take longer to achieve successes, whereas men are found to be climbing up the ladder faster. The main reason for the almost stagnant growth of women in corporate field is ego pertaining amongst the coworkers.

  This can be set right with multiple solutions, but with only one effective solution of 'accepting that we all are equal, and recognition and growth should occur to the well-deserving human, may it be woman or man'.

- **Office Politics** – Where there are people there is politics. Discrimination based on the way you look, the way you dress, being a fresher, being an introverted and lack of experience, gender, societal status, and most importantly if you are a married/lactating mother, is widely noted in all institutions and this is called as office politics.

  The generosity a woman deserves from her coworkers is undeniably necessary for a woman to grow mentally and in terms of her career. Office politics plays a disastrous role in deterring a person from exhibiting their complete honest self towards the institution.

Often ganging up against an individual who is incapable of speaking up for themselves, leads to mental health issues, which in turn affects the performance capabilities of that individual.

I have personally witnessed how playing little office game monopoly hurts the emotions of a person and harms them mentally. Having a safe space where one feels comfortable to open up about newer ideas and goals, makes an individual and a company grow effectively.

Addressing to only a certain section of people whilst making corporate decisions, favoring the opinions of an individual who has just the same knowledge and experience as the other, because of some professional/ personal bias, and many such incidents leads to office politics in smaller scale. This goes unnoticeable at times whereas sometimes becomes the root cause of problems for an employee.

Some level of compromise, negotiation, and politicking is acceptable and can be ignored too. But this gets tricky and problematic when the personal goals and organizational goals don't go together. The personal motivation of causing hurt intentionally, takes the front row seat.

To resolve an issue arising out of conflict of office politics, firstly, all the coworkers need to accept that workplace is a shared space for every individual, a company welcomes into. The senior most member from the hierarchy has to impart and implement the true sense of equality among office men. The rooted discrimination based on gender, newly hired, and physical performance has to be extracted out. Although workplace politics are inevitable, they can be overcome with proper leadership and influence.

The exertion of power is explicitly unbearable. Such behavior is inevitable, given that human beings are naturally political and will do whatever it takes to protect their own interests.

Workplace politics can be positive or negative. Your responsibility as a leader is to avoid and overcome the negative political behavior in your workplace.

- **Unrecognized Efforts at Workplace** – Being a woman, not getting enough recognition at workplace in a corporate world, doesn't have to really shocking. At times, when I put forth my project-specific idea, it was overheard by other panel members during a meeting. Polished and painted over my same idea by another male colleague was appreciated and accepted with applaud. This is something every working woman faces and yet can't help being powerless and voiceless.

It not only hurts mentally, but also shreds confidence off a woman or any person for that sake. Promotions, raise in pay and recognition in the corporate forefront is desired by every person since the day 1 of their joining. Equal recognition for the work and efforts is definitely not a lot to ask for.

Recognition, equal treatment, annual raise and honor are all intertwined. Loss or lack in one sector will drag you down the lane of progress. Exclusion comes at a great cost to organizations in the form of lowered job satisfaction, reduced work effort, diminished employee voice, and greater intention to leave. Building an inclusive workplace means creating a culture that fully engages and supports all employees.

You cannot grow as a leader unless you embrace new challenges that stretch your thinking beyond your comfort zone. You become an inspirational leader when you have the humility to build a team with people more talented than you.

This problem can be tackled mainly by putting aside the male ego generated in tiny little empty office spaces. Exhibiting and implementing the true sense of involving all the teammates and treating them with equal attention and carefully listening to the unique perspectives and ideas put forth will help company progress, whilst ignoring the negative factor of leaving a person's efforts offshore.

- **Biased Pay scale** – Most women like me, working in the corporate field have faced lots of discrimination based on gender, nationality, caste, and pay. Biased pay scale is justified in many institutions by saying that men contribute more when compared to women, considering the things that keep pulling women back such as getting married and moving to a place, pregnancy, post-partum leave, and constant health issues after all this.

An opinion that is widely propaganded but will never be accepted by the male dominated work places is that, 'they believe that men are long term assets to the company than women with same experience and wisdom'. This opinion is rooted in our society for such a long time now, that it doesn't even seem stigmatized. An Underpaid woman employee is a product of a society which is mind-fed by the 'Men are more capable than women' society.

Studies have showcased that around two-third working population of women have lacked to set a woman role model for themselves to look up to. A lack of senior or visibly successful female role models as a major obstacle to their career advancement has been recorded constantly.

Due to an unequal pay when compared with men, women seem to feel put down at workplace, which ends up wrecking their career. The global report shows that four in every 10 women see the gender pay gap as a key issue, with women in seven nations listing this discrepancy as their major concern.

53% of working Indian women have faced harassment at workplace. Unequal pay can also be put in the category of mental harassment. Personally, being a women, I know that women seize the big-shot opportunities instantly, when found.

On an average, every corporate company house over 25% of female population now. But still unfortunately, women who do choose to pursue a career are often faced with considerable challenges. These include pervasive stereotypes about their abilities and skills, higher stress and anxiety compared to women working in different fields, and lack of career advancement opportunities.

This bias can be overcome gradually with generational propaganda of equality in all institutions. Voicing the oppressed female when your voice is heard will help restore faith in sisterhood/ brotherhood even in workplace.

- **Delayed Promotion** - Women who have worked in male-dominated spaces, have always felt left-out, denied/ of promotion, turned down on opinions, talked over, ignored, denied of equal pay and many more.

Researches show that women tend to climb up the career ladder slower when compared to men. It is mostly connected with the stigma attached to 'that time of the month', when you end up in a heated argument with your colleague... Instead of putting a valid explanation ahead of you, they end up asking if you're menstruating. There's no doubt that we women experience changes in moods and abdominal cramps, which in turn results is lesser functionality of women. But this doesn't define her capability to work. Nor should her health condition be used against her to put down her efforts and recognition.

A person's inputs to the corporate institute is calculated on an average basis and not scrutinized on a daily basis. The promotion should ne honored to the person who truly has been as asset to the company throughout the year and not just today. Impeccable assets are those 'who considers work as their own responsibility and not just work'. Who understands work and responsibility all together, better than a woman? A WOMAN.

Promotion should be conferred to the one that is the most deserving. The best way to keep this whole yearly promotions transparent is by setting up a team, consisting of all the unbiased members of the company, who would make the appropriate, fair and transparent system of promoting the one that truly deserves the raise up the ladder.

- **Lessened Opportunities** – Women tend to have lesser exposure and opportunities in the major work forces of the country. Majorly because of all the stigma like poor work-life balance, postpartum phase, being a new mother in the race of progression.

Women tend to face harassment mentally, sexually regularly in workplaces. Opportunities automatically gets lessened with an idea that India is not safe for working women. Late night shifts, prolonged working hours, dank roads while returning from work and unnoticed competition among men and women to hunt down a position at work, decreases the available opportunities for her.

You can be an effective leader by talking on women's behalf, standing up for the betterment of their conditions at work, gang up occasionally and inculcate among them the importance of self-defense. Narrate to them your success story, because they will need a role model to look up to and keep going. Go an extra mile and help them get a cab service back home, if their work timing is longer than the usual.

Since COVID-19 pandemic hit the world, it has caused disastrous effects on the human lives. But it has kind of been a boon to the whole sector of working women. It enhanced the flexibility for newly lactating mothers, pregnant employees of the institute to work from home comfortably.

Another reason for lessened opportunities sometimes for women in corporate, is because of lack of required and valuable knowledge, poor communication, anti-social behavior, and zero to very low self-confidence. You being a leader can definitely help them have a great office experience by making them feel 'they matter'.

- **Constant Failures** – Some women tend to feel that 'quitting even before trying' is the easiest way of not having to tackle with failures. This feeling is mostly because of their previous traumatizing experience of failures in interviews, or basic hiring processes.

An effective leader will make sure they overcome from their gut that holds them back from functioning their 100% and their potential goes untapped. Make sure that they receive incentives, bonuses and recognitions on time with enough appreciation of being an asset to the company. Make them realize their worth by putting them up in a situation from which the only way to get out will be to face it.

Tell them that failures are a part of life. Failures are caused for several reasons… one of them is because of not putting 100% effort and another would actually be lack of required expertise and knowledge for the job. Help them figure out their reason for failure and on how to overtake their fears the next time.

A famous quote always read that, "Failure is not the opposite of success, it's a part of success". Spread awareness about importance on mental health and that there are always people to whom they matter. A leader will never leave his/her fellowmen in times of difficulty.

- **Fear of losing the current job** – The current profile is always at stake for every average household earning person. The pressure is doubled in size if the earning person is a woman. The current global labor force participation rate for women is just under 47%. For men, it's 72%. That's a difference of 25 percentage points, with some regions facing a gap of more than 50 percentage points.

Around the world, finding a job is much tougher for women than it is for men. When women are employed, they tend to work in low-quality jobs in vulnerable conditions, and there is little improvement forecast in the near future.

Women tend to fall back in the race mostly because of lack of keeping up and adapting with the constantly changing environment around them. May it be technology, parental responsibilities, post-partum phase, lactating conditions and many more things require constant up gradation.

The competition in the corporate world is mostly not among who is the most accurate, deserving and promising candidate for the top corporate positions. It is among Men and women as a whole. No matter how much we impart the knowledge of equality, women and men can never function the same.

The most accurate and best thing to be done as a leader is to ensure that women working in your institution have their positions at work secured. This can be done by helping them be updated regularly with work, world affairs and current requirements in the field of work. By providing them with weekend classes for soft skills improvement, technical classes or on how to socialize at workplace.

"Always remember that leadership is a privilege. When you're in a leadership role, your influence may affect the trajectories of people's entire careers and often their lives."

- **Distorted Work-life balance** – We always end up expecting women to be great at multi-tasking, managing everything flawlessly at work and at home. To manage kids, married life, work and health should be considered equally applicable to both men and women.

I although strongly believe that the nature has created Men and women different on numerous terms but they do function similar to each other. There is no such thing at a workplace wherein a woman is deemed to be incapable of handling, other than the shallow mindsets of certain anti-feminists. But men by default are only expected to be handling their work life seriously and the responsibility of nurturing a family is directly upon women, even though it puts her career at stake.

Why is it always expected out of women to have a much sorted work-life balance and to carry the entire burden graciously? While the work can be equally distributed between the partners at home and at work, they can perform their best by having little helps of flexible and comfortable work hours and not being treated in a biased way.

The typical mindset that women are best suited for being a home maker alone has not changed much. In order to provide the financial aid to the family and to have herself occupied and have a prestigious life, a woman chooses to work, although nothing comes easy for her as it is for her male counterpart. Instead of her efforts being valued, it is seen as if she was born with the audacity that she cares less for her family. This needs to change effectively.

This can be changed gradually by imparting that women deserve to be treated with utmost respect, dignity and honor. Her efforts should be recognized both at workplace and home. Every person knows at least one woman around them who has complained and seemed disappointed for being treated anything less than men and for their almost failed marriage because they focused on their career.

When the kids grow up and turn out anything unexpected by their family, the entire blame is put on the mother who sacrificed her personal precious time with her kid, just so she could also provide the luxurious life, that she couldn't have. The graph of being treated bad, doesn't seem to be going down unless serious changes in internal values are made. Being an effective leader, one should profess the importance of an environment where equity and equality both matter.

- **Existence of Male Ego** – Another important challenge faced by working women from corporate is having ego clashes with their partner and/or at workplace. This topic doesn't receive much attention as it should. Talking about it makes this a very ignorant topic by giving the most lamest excuse that, 'Men were manufactured that way', which makes it clear that there is a white translucent curtain in between, that everyone can see, but will never talk about.

A study published in the Journal of Personality and Social Psychology, found that men's implicit self-esteem was negatively affected by their romantic partner's success. Meanwhile, women remained unaffected by their partner's performance and success. It was also noted that, having a partner who experiences a success might hurt men's implicit self-esteem, ambition and success.

We might imagine two possible outcomes for self-esteem resulting from a romantic partner's success. On one hand, a partner's success could lead to an increase in self-esteem, and could go down terribly in another scenario.

Women before finalizing the man to spend their entire life with, need to exclusively have this topic discussed in depth. About how would they support her through her career goals, failures, and significant growth? Having his conversation will have him guilty every time he puts your career down and that solves the problem of ego between the partners.

Researchers have found also that men tend to exaggerate their agented traits, whereas women tend to exaggerate communal traits. To the extent that competence is central to men's self-perceptions than to women's, men's self-esteem is more likely to be negatively affected when their competence is in question.

The gender bias at workplace also makes space for ego clashes and changed behavior towards the female counterpart at work. Even though women decide to break of the stereotypical mindset of being treated bad and different, the implications later on will sure land them in a complicated place. Women are expected to underplay and under-perform so as to not irk their male counterpart's ego.

Work politics, Male ego clashes are inevitable, it can still be overcome by having an effective leadership in place. A good leader will make sure to put things in place so as to create an environment that is friendly and interesting.

- **Safety and Dignity** – Its 2022 and women in India still feel unsafe for working till late at night. Women move away from families and parents in order to find a job that they're happy with. But with India, around 44% of the working women population feel unsafe post 6 PM. Only 42 per cent of women admitted that better pay package is an attraction for working during night while rest said they had no other choice.

Working to meet the family's financial needs is one thing, but working for the same with honor and dignity is something every woman looks out for, in a corporate job.

The typical orthodox mindset of the society has not changed much, which is another major bad influence on the working women. The way they look at a woman who returns home after a tiring day at work, is as though they're returning after committing a crime. There have been instances of verbal abuses from the societal neighbors, house owners and cab drivers. When all they were doing is, earning a living for themselves.

Every person in this country has to the right to practice the profession they like. While men are considered hardworking and sacrificial at the same time for working late, women get abused and treated unequal. This sense of inequality has to be rooted out of our systems. I personally believe that, women can never be called equal to men, because they both have their own sets of strengths and weaknesses. Calling them equal on all levels, would be mere 'ignoring the facts'.

Many a times, you won't even be aware of the situation, a woman is in if she's taking the extra mile to work beyond her regular hours. Some could be single mothers, newly divorced woman or someone who's doing it because she likes to work passionately. What is wrong if someone is working out of passion?

The dignity and honor, is something that a woman deserves, even if she is into a profession that you dislike or disapprove of.

'Her profession does not define the amount of respect, you give her'.

The freedom to work by choice, in conditions of dignity, safety and fairness – is integral to human welfare. Guaranteeing that women have access to this right is an important end in itself. A woman's personal preference is the key factor in determining whether she will seek out and engage in corporate work.

Effective leaders at corporate should emphasize on keeping the dignity, honor, and respect of women. Workplaces also have an equal part to play in the betterment of dignity of women in their respective spaces. Providing for a safer environment to work, assigning people and committees to look into the issues and grievances of the one who have been mistreated.

- **No ownership on her own earning** – Humans work hard with an intention of getting paid well to meet the financial needs of their families. In most cases witnessed so far, men and women have had their share of meeting the running needs of the family.

But somehow it is expected out of a woman that she has no rights over her own earnings, as to spend something for her self-care.

It is an act of generosity, and breaking the stereotypical mindset of women bound to be suitable only for house-making. This decision should be honored and respected by her families. This mindset will not be developed overnight.. It is a process, which could take months, years or maybe never. But as far as my opinion is concerned 'No matter how much it takes, one should never stop trying to bring in about changes".

When a woman starts working, it is obviously to benefit herself and to improve the financial status of the family to meet the sustainability and be a helping hand to her father before getting married, to husband later on. Spending on herself or investing in something that she believes is an asset should be heard, processed and then be accepted by her family. Her decisions should be respected with utmost care and honor.

Honoring a woman in your life, may it be your mother, sister, wife, daughter or even a female colleague will only reflect on how well you were brought up. It defines the amount of perseverance in doing certain things. As an effective leader, one should know how sensitive and important this topic is, and to discuss it and create awareness among your coworkers on how and why it is to know that the financial needs being met by her, is an act of kindness and that she can absolutely spend it wherever and however deemed necessary.

- **Sexual Harassment** – Women have been facing sexual harassment at workplace for several years now. It has become such a topic that everyone is aware of and also has cracked multiple solutions to address it, but has still failed to uproot it.

Harassment is not just seen to be sexually, as we discussed previously, it is verbally in meetings, physically while travelling to and from work etc. Most women tend to ignore them all and still move on with their work with a strong intention of supporting her family amidst all the harassment.

This treatment towards a woman who's taking the extra mile to make her ends meet so her family sustains a healthy, happy living, is inacceptable and unbearable in all forms. From handling the judgmental looks of the society to getting abused brutally at work, when a woman returns home for a peaceful dinner, she gets abused even there when she fails to attend to the needs of her child or husband on a very farther level.

Women working late in the night face a lot of sexual harassment. Corporate companies have put forth many solutions as to prevent the harassment till certain level and also they allow the victim to lodge the grievance complaint from within the surveillance of company too.

Women are well known for ignoring and fighting silent wars within themselves. Most women deal with all sorts of mistreatments silently in order to not lose the job that is feeding them. But continuous bearing od this treatment will only make the opponent stronger and will make her lose the leftover self-confidence, self-respect and dignity she has been preserving for years now.

Being a leader, make sure you create a safer environment for women around you to function productively whilst feeling safe and protected. Every woman deserves a life filled with pride, honor, dignity and respect from her male counterpart and colleagues at workplace.

It took a disturbing incident like the Delhi's Nirbhaya case, to start speaking up about the harassments faced by them. Even now women prefer staying silent about the harassments they face rather than talking out about it and wrecking their careers.

Nearly one third of women interviewed admit to having experienced harassment, although more than 60% do not report it. Indian women are the most likely to speak up (53%), a clear change of attitude can be noticed since 2012.

Sexual harassment can happen on many levels about the appearance, choices, mode of work, dressing sense and many such things. The sexual harassment numbers have gone high since women decided to talk and share their experience with the outer world. A leader should create a common space which feels comfortable, open and secure for anybody to come out and talk.

CHAPTER 3

How To Climb Up Corporate Ladder, Faster

Women have long suffered for gaining equal opportunities in corporate world. Growing faster and having a career of their own is a dream of million women out there. This generation of millennials have a diverse way of working, as they believe that working for one company throughout, reduces their career growth and suffocates them of the same environment, unlike our older generation practiced sacrificing their career growth and white labelled it as 'Faithfulness.'

"The culture has changed and people no longer stay at one firm for the entirety of their career," says Ford Myers, a career coach and author of get the job you want, even when no one's hiring.

The growth in corporate ladder has a significant thing to be noted.. Growth need not be straight up vertically, it can be lateral or parallel, but will get you at a far better place than a vertical ladder.

Haven't we all heard this piece of advice from our senior coworkers that, "It took me these many years to where I am today, hence you will require same amount of time to reach here too"? We can officially declare that there is no such need to struggle patiently for those many years to climb up the corporate ladder anymore. Millennials have proved this by their constant ability to exhibit impatience by switching jobs. Growth is a natural sign of being alive, so it is healthy to want to expand, develop, and advance both personally and professionally.

Women although find it harder to place themselves up in a position that most people look up to. Mostly because of the discrimination rooted by the society in all the young minds. Being an effective corporate leader, immaterial of the thorns put your way, you ease their way up.

Growth defines a person's psychological ability to lead a successful and greedless life. Being an effective leader, you try and help your team members to makes the accessibility easier. Make it a priority to appreciate your team and most importantly, thank them in frequent intervals for their inputs to the company.

Let us now discuss in detail, on how to grow in corporate, faster...

- **Make a Plan** – "Know where you're headed", this phrase right here puts light on the critical topic of "Know and acknowledge your path, before actually walking on it". This helps you have you destination and goal clearly stuck in your head while you feel like backing off.

  On days when you're questioning on why you are working it all off, you will find the answers in your chaos. Setting up a plan and having a goal, will help you reach wherever you're manifesting to be in the next 5-10 years.

  Another main reason why one should have an elaborated plan is because, along the way to a certain destination, we get to measure the amount of success, by celebrating little victories and embracing setbacks towards the victories.

  When we talk about putting out a detailed plan, it also includes one's personal life goals too. These gains in corporate world, need not necessarily hurt your personal life growth. Some growths are intertwined, like saving up or investing in buying property with the financial gains from work.

  Setting goals are vital to your career success, but knowing how to set goals is also critically important. It's one thing to state a goal and another to be able to set a goal that is attainable and realistic. Unrealistic expectations and goal-setting can harm your mental peace, when you fail in reaching them eventually.

  Before you start goal setting, consider doing a self-assessment to help you determine some parameters for your goal setting. Self-assessment on what are your strengths and weaknesses, on how to keep up with growing technologically advancing world.

If you want to be a leader, give your team the space to work, create an environment free from the impediments of toxicity and witness a significant growth in your company but, more importantly, in your team.

A leader who cares about the growth of their company along with the employees, should make sure to give an ear and provide them with solutions while they come to you seeking help. Putting them and their ideas down will only result in them, losing their self-confidence in all matters.

Make yourself an example that people would want to look up to, no matter how hard you've struggled to be wherever you are. Give them inputs on how they can make their goals and destination reasonable. "Life is what happens when you're busy making other plans". You can't predict the future, so be flexible about your goals so they can adapt as necessary. Also be sure to review them on occasion to see if they need adjusting to new circumstances.

- **Keep Networking** – "Networking never ends", even when you have a job that satisfies your wants and needs, networking should never be stopped. The more you know people, the more it is likely to help you climb up the corporate ladder. Most people stop involving in talks with other department colleagues and friends who have gotten in to different portfolios. But this means you are headed in the opposite direction of effective networking.

You never know, which resource of yours will place you with another higher position in corporate. Which is why it is told to "keep your resourceful people close and in good proximity".

Keep talking to people about your goals and get inputs from different perspectives. Talking to older set of people, will get you an experienced angle, while talking to a younger colleague will help you gain a fresh and collective perspective.

Networking will help a wide set of people know how capable of a person you are. It will give them an idea of your strengths, plans, goals and intention of growing up the corporate ladder. Although these sets of advice becomes more crucial if a female employee wills to ramp up her career, since the discrimination based on many factors like gender bias, come in between most of the times. While it is seen and observed to be easier for a male employee than it is for his female counterpart.

As an effective leader, you understand the grass root level challenges standing in between an employee and their goal. Help them enlarge their networking zone by introducing them to the influential and experienced employees from your end.

"No one can be a great leader unless they genuinely care about the success of everyone on their team."

Guide them well on how to increase the networking and speak about their wants, needs, strengths and experience. Impart that having multiple perspectives will only land them in a position of better experience and satisfaction of job.

- **Work Hard and Work Smart** – "Know the fine line between Hard-work and Smart-work". Coming from a corporate world, I indulge with many activities and deal with different sets of people who have taught this most important lesson in my life that, "Smart work pays off better than hard work". We have all come across this term called 'Smart-work', atleast once in our entire lives. What does it actually mean? It simply means to do any job effectively with minimal efforts.

It isn't rocket science to understand that any work can be custom-changed according to one's ability of doing it. Some people believe that the systematic way of doing it is the only way out. But only a smart person will show you how it is done systematically and with little efforts. Be that person. "Remember that there are multiple ways of reaching to you goal, choose your goal wisely".

As we already spoke, make both short-term and long-term realistic goals. You need both. Short-term goals can be easier to set and achieve. Long-term goals give you a big picture view of your ultimate goals. Setting short-term goals can keep you motivated as you achieve them, and they should help you to eventually accomplish your long-term goal.

Work on your project for extra hours, considering which time of the day, you're most productive. Be that person, people will seek help from with respect to your work. Team members should have your name on the tip of their tongues, because, when they need you, they know that you'll be there for them. Start aligning the company needs with that of your personal needs. Start dreaming big and smart for yourself.

Outdo yourself from the last day's YOU. Try and be better everyday. Remember that the competition is within yourself and with the outer world you're dealing with. "You never know if you can do it, unless you actually do it."

"Poor leadership is building a great team and doing everything in your power to hold onto control. It makes no sense to recruit the best people and tie their hands by not giving them the freedom to perform."

An effective leader can help people by lowering the pressure on one person and rather distribute it evenly among the employees. And to create a challenging environment at work, while the employees will be left with no choice than outdoing themselves every single time. Although this seems like a task that's a little overboard to being realistic, but can still be achieved by following it properly.

- **Dream Beyond the Job Description** – We can also simply put this as, "work for something that doesn't come as part of your responsibility". More often, the people who think out of the box, show extraordinary skills, and who exhibits the true sense of working even outside their comfort zone, end up in better positions in life.

This simply talks about how dynamic and versatile, the corporate world expects you to be. And to grow in a surrounding like that, you have to always be someone with better experience in all the fields, basically a little more than what your job description asks for.

Develop an "I will do whatever it takes to get the job done" attitude.

I strongly believe that, your work attitude is just as important as your work aptitude. Most people work hard, but if you're the one with the can-do attitude, your supervisor will certainly recognize and appreciate it. And with this attitude, when you lay down a plan for climbing high, the people who've known your skills, will stand supportive to you. This does not mean ignoring present responsibilities; it means working beyond achievements that are obvious or expected.

Setting up limits for yourself is good, but don't end up binding yourself up in these limits. Limits are meant to monitor an individual's capacity, and not to limit their growth in career. In corporate world, most institutions expects an employee to work by pouring full productivity, leading to the betterment of the company and the individual herself.

Treat everything with urgency and volunteer for high-visibility projects. Always seek to contribute more, and be known as the go-to person or the get-it-done person, he adds. "Arrive earlier and leave later. There is no replacement for hard work and smart work."

Myers says. "Do more than most people, and work harder and longer."

Being a leader, help make the safe space, wherein people, including women find it comfortable and safe if they choose to pitch in more hours at workplace. Arrange for seminars and conferences where people who have accomplished a good satisfactory life. Help them motivate thousands of people looking up at them and you.

- **Be an asset to the company** – Any corporate company hires an employee with an intention that ahead in future, this person's inputs might be fruitful. They start looking at you as an asset, which is an expected criteria for an employer in corporate world. It is expected automatically out of an employee to perform their best and contribute to the company

Keep yourself updated by upgrading your skill set needed in the corporate world. Considering how rapidly the world is witnessing changes, it is rather helpful for personal growth and also to the company you're providing your inputs for. Try breaking out and getting out of your zone and boundaries.

"Your growth is defined by the boundaries you set for yourself." Read, know, and inculcate the necessary qualities needed to be one among the many who are running the race with you. Make your identity distinguishable from the other entire set of teammates. Stand out being extra-ordinarily abled. Work for the betterment of yourself silently, whilst you work louder for the corporate growth of the company.

"Growth and development of people is the highest calling of leadership."

Present yourself in a way, as if you were presenting the entire company. The way you dress, the way you speak, walk, work, eat, sit and laugh everything needs to be modified in accordance with, what and where you want to be in a company. A quote read, "Don't look at how your peers are dressed; look at how the top executives are dressed. Dress for the position you want, not the one you have".

Try and understand your company in a better way. Especially read the ones on top of you, in the hierarchy. Understand their goals, and expected outcomes from the employees in a better way and implement it in your working methods. Align your modus operandi with that of the company's you're working for.

Every leader, manager or boss needs lieutenants, and when you serve them their favors, you will increase and they are likely to pull you in and up to more responsibility and opportunities for quicker advancement.

As an effective leader, put forth the ideas, goals and expectations of a company from its employees, this type of advancement is rather helpful during the initial stages of employee training. Help them figure out their goals towards the corporate ladder. Educate them on how crucial, the quantifiable details are - Bosses like measurable, quantifiable results, "If you can't provide that in your review, you're just another employee begging for a raise or promotion."

- **Think and act a level above** – It is all a psychological thinking, which involves thinking and acting like someone from up in the hierarchy of work. It is always appreciated for an employee to think, act, and take decisions as if he was a member of the higher deciding committee in a company, who gets the make the decisions.

Behaving, talking, debating, thinking from a farther vision, just like the one functioning above your level would do. Not everyone gets to think and act like their superior one, but I can assure that, this is a quality that every employee with an intention of growing high, can inculcate at any point in time.

Observe closely on what are the qualities that you lack as an employee, but the one above you masters at? Know it and dig deep in to learn those new qualities that will help train your mind and indulge in a psychology equal to that of your boss. Pay attention to how those above you act, manage, delegate, mentor and communicate, and emulate their behavior. What skills have they mastered? Learn those skills.

Be keenly aware of broader company goals. Know which projects are being funded, who is in charge of those projects, what priorities are high and which ones are low.

"Align yourself with the people and projects at the highest levels of attention and expectation. This gives you visibility and the chance to shine more quickly." Someone who is fully in charge and fully responsible for his or her own career is more likely to make good decisions and succeed.

An effective leader will talk closely with the management and organize a monthly or quarterly check-up workshops at workplace that will train the employees in tapping the best resource inputs from within themselves. Ask the one looking up at you, to be an initiator, not just an executor.

- **Be a team player** – It is very keenly looked upon and learnt that, an employee that is being hired for a company in corporate world, will always be under observation as to see how good and effective of a team player he/she is. No matter how much of a leadership qualities one possess, an employee is always expected to be a great team player.

  Employers constantly have an eye on every employee on how well they're interacting with other team members and other department colleagues. A major factor that influences the assessment of an employee in terms of raising up on the career ladder, is if he/she is good at team management and team work. If your assessment says you are a good team player, it is definitely taking you to places in future. That assessment report will talk on your behalf on the day of promotion. "The ability to win friends and influence others is a skill needed increasingly as you move up in any organization."

  A "team" is not just people who work at the same time in the same place. A real team is a group of very different individuals who enjoy working together and who share a commitment to working cohesively to help the organization achieve their common goals and fulfill its purpose.

  Remember to always be grateful for all the opportunities extended towards you, be it by offering you to head the presentation in conference, or to handle higher level delegates. Always be thankful, you never know what little gesture of yours will attract your company CEO official.

  A good leader will always help her/ his team members be practical and aware of current happenings in the company. When possible and practical, support people in working remotely, and allow them to work hours that make sense for their lives outside of work. Creative solutions such as job sharing (having multiple people share one role), virtual work teams, and sabbatical options can help employers find the best talent no matter where or when they need to work.

Many leaders seem to forget that leading others should be held in reverence more than anything else. Being the leader means that you have been placed in a position to serve others. Leaders are only as successful as their teams, and the great ones know that with the right team dynamics, decisions, and diverse personalities, in place, everyone wins.

Too often, I have seen leaders duck and cover, throw their people under the bus, and throw their positional weight around, and instead of leading from a place of service, lead from a place of ego when things get rough.

You are privileged to be in a position where you can direct, shape, and focus people's potential toward a specific result. When you are given the responsibility to lead, you are given an awesome opportunity to influence the lives of many people positively, a responsibility you should never take for granted.

"We are not a team because we work together, we are a team because we respect, trust, and care for each other."

Remember that employees working under great leadership are happier, more productive and more connected to their organizations. This has a ripple effect that is always reflected back on the organizational growth.

"You become a true leader, when you help your team become successful. Remember leadership is not about you, it is all about the people you serve."

CHAPTER 4

Powerful Body Language – Courage To Act And Dare To Lead

Many a times, when we talk about the technicalities and challenges pertaining to the working women, we miss out on talking about how salient is the 'Body language'. This comes as part of developing soft skills within oneself. Our bodies tend to exhibit and talk non-verbally in a language of its own. Sometimes to an extent of exposing your inner self and the type of leader you are.

It sets up an impeccable image of yours in the minds of your coworkers, boss, and the people who look up to you. In case you are avoiding paying attention to what you're speaking non-verbally, you are sabotaging your own career at a slow pace.

Developing of soft skills is not an overnight process, but a process that comes with constant efforts and practice. Mastering the art of the non-verbal communication, more importantly than the oral/ verbal communication, is very significant in all terms.

Exhibiting powerful body language is an art that needs to be closely paid attention to, but yet remains the least paid-attention topic by corporate individuals. Being a leader, and possessing the leader-like qualities are two different things.

Women in corporate sector are often misinterpreted as being submissive and not decisive. This is not because they are incapable of handling the leadership and guide the ones in need, but because of the non-verbal they do out of their actions, the body language. The only constraint that pulls them back from acquiring the higher level posts.

The most ignorable of actions of women tend to create an impression that women are weak, incapable, and rather emotional. It could be the tone of the expression, the way you communicate, and lot many factors. It all adds up to be the body language being the most crucial factor.

Everybody talks. And *every body* talks, too. We don't even need to say a thing because our bodies can reveal details about our thoughts and feelings in a flash.

Body language allows us to connect better and more easily with the people around you and convey your expertise and authority without saying a word. When you are genuinely listening to the other person, they can tell, and it makes the connection exponentially stronger. Powerful body language makes you feel more confident. Consider how you take up space and consider using power poses to make you feel and be perceived as more confident.

We are going to discuss the set of most influential and significant set of body languages that will take you to newer heights.

Let us just go ahead and discuss it –

- **Right Facial expression** – The quote has it saying, "Face is the index of mind", it really is. What's on your mind, will show up on your face. Negative thoughts, fear, excitement, and misery have all found a different way of exhibiting themselves on your face.

  It is about how and what you are expressing out, you need not have an ever-smiling face with an intention of impressing a panel of coworkers. Express your disagreements, keep your point, address a conference full of people, and do everything that seems necessary, but finding the right amount of the expression is an art that has to be inculcated and applied in right amounts.

  It's your job to manage the mood and demeanor that you bring into a room. Having a go-to facial expression can help you regulate your behavior and by extension of your own feelings, since you'll give yourself time to consider the situation at hand rather than simply reacting to it.

  Avoiding eye contact may cause implications like lack of interest, and acknowledgement of the person's efforts, who's presenting in front of you. If you are the one talking, looking down as you talk makes it seem like you lack confidence or are self-conscious, causing your words to lose their effect. It's especially important to keep your eyes level if you're making complicated or important points.

Continuous eye contact, establishes a sense of strong leadership, confidence and strength. Complete negligence will clearly have negative effects on your professional relationships. 'Rolling eyes', when showing disinterest, is also another major faulty approach towards a better body language. You are communicating disinterest, while the other person feels less confident, which doesn't really make you an effective leader.

Women are most likely to feel ignored, avoided, and receive all the rolling eyes treatment, avoidance of eye contact while they speak in the corporate. All one can do to improvise the situation is to just be kind and to be empathetic.

- **Power of 'Power Poses'** – We must have heard since our schooling on why and how important it is to maintain certain decent posture that illuminates the power, interest, confidence, strength, and an idea of you being an effective leader.

As much as facial expressions are important, perfect body postures are quintessential for expressing a powerful body language. We can basically tell good body language is a high power pose while, a poor body language is a low power pose. High-power poses, like outstretched arms, express confidence and strength while low power poses, such as a hunched back, express protection and increase feelings of stress.

Folded arms, slouched neck and a questionably uncomfortable pose, you are sending a signal to your coworker that you are shy, unconfident, and uncomfortable. As a leader, this should not be one of the signals you'll be sending out to the people who're looking up to you. High-power poses, like outstretched arms, express confidence and strength.

Clenched fists, much like crossed arms and legs, can signal that you're not open to other people's points. It can also make you look argumentative and defensive, which will make people nervous about interacting with you, making you an ineffective leader.

If you're smiling or are engaged in a pleasant conversation, the other person may get a nagging sense that you're shutting him or her out. Even if folding your arms feels comfortable, resist the urge to do so if you want people to see you as open-minded and interested in what they have to say.

Throwing out your low power posing capabilities and inculcating and adapting to the higher power poses should not seem very difficult. Practicing high power poses in front of your colleagues not only imparts confidence in others, but also makes you confident and a leader who's worth taking risks and going an extra mile for your coworkers.

- **Indulge in Active Listening** – Humans tend to lose interest all of a sudden after a certain while, it is worse in cases where the listening goes on for long. Finding a way to keep the conversation interesting and attractive is one way of pulling the audience once they've just lost the interest. Being a listener is as essential as being an effective speaker. Listening is a skill, a leader is expected to possess even if the topic being discussed is out of your interest.

Nodding at correct times, is one way of expressing your agreement and submission to the decisions being made. But at the same time, the rooted difference between a woman's nod and a man's nod, makes it difficult to understand the science behind nodding. The best advice with respect to nodding, is to nod specifically only when you're agreeing and to stay firm while a serious discussion is underway and to have an expression that addresses the curiosity of the topic.

An effective leader, is expected to hear and address to the problems, ideas, and thoughts from his/her coworker. This comes purely with an art of listening well and carefully. History has it, listeners have achieved more than what speakers have.

"Speakers, speak experiences, while listeners adopt speakers' experiences."

In order to practice active listening body language, you need to deeply analyze when you need to listen and when you can give feedback. You need to determine if you are providing value to a conversation or simply interrupting inappropriately because you're not really listening to what the other person has to say.

Use head tilts when you want to demonstrate your concern for and interest in members of your team, or when you want to encourage people to expand on what they are saying. But when you need to project power and authority, you should keep your head straight up in a more neutral position.

Simple things help: Sit up, keep eye contact, use open movements while gesturing, and keep your fingertips lightly touching while resting your hands. Listening, relating, connecting emotionally – these are the values to express with your non-verbal communication.

- **Firm Handshakes** – The simplest of the non-verbal communication is 'Firm handshakes'. Not too hard, not too loose, we call the firm handshakes as the key to mastering the non-verbal communication. This speaks a lot about your body language being either condescending, or respectful or just right at your position. And that is decided by the strength of your handshakes.

It is hidden within such a seemingly simple formality as an opportunity to make a lasting impression. Here's how you can be good at it - When shaking hands, look directly into the other person's eyes, Smile, Stand when being introduced to someone and when extending your hand, Make sure your right hand is free to shake hands. Always shift any briefcases, papers, beverages or cell phones to your left hand before you begin the greeting so your hand is ready for action.

Keep yourself fully attentive, especially when being introduced to a person that creates an impression as you're respectful and interested. Make sure you have palm-to-palm contact and that the web of your hand touches the web of the other person's.

Offer your hand pointing sideways always, as this sends a message of your submissiveness. Whereas, when someone gives their palm pointing downwards, it shows their superiority. But people who offer a sideways hand to shake send a message of equality and confidence.

The thing to keep in mind is that the purpose of a handshake at work is to greet someone or say good-bye or express congratulations or to signal agreement on a deal. As such, it should be perceived as warm, friendly, and sincere.

This goes differently with men and women. Women offer for a handshake, they're considered as too condescending and demanding. But if they don't they're seen as fragile and uninterested. This works differently although, but the firmness in handshakes is something that can be learnt, adapted and experienced.

- **Talk with your hands** – Research has proven that, gesturing while you talk, improves the clarity of your speech. Immaterial of how and what you want to convey, leaning against the wall, simply speaking it out with loads of fillers won't make you an effective speaker or presenter. The movements of hands while talking steals the show, as you're expected to be using less filler words like 'umm' and 'uhh'.

Since gesture is integrally linked to speech, gesturing as you talk can actually power up your thinking. Start practicing 'I have nothing to hide', attitude by displaying and resting your arms on the table when one of your colleagues is presenting or talking with you. That shows your openness as a leader and freeness for others to open up around you.

Individuals with open gestures are perceived more positively and are more persuasive than those with closed gestures (arms crossed, hands hidden or held close to the body, etc.) Also, if you hold your arms at waist level, and gesture within that plane, most audiences will perceive you as assured and credible.

This is applicable for both men and women. Expressing with your hand movements only makes you a better speaker, and inhibits the thought of holding back, shying away or refraining from being the best version of yourself.

- **Look out for Vocal Pitch** – This plays a very important role in the way you will be perceived at your workplace. You voice pitch decides on how much of a condescending person you are. The intention is not to talk soft or high, it is to talk with right amount of pitch. To be able to modulate the tone and pitch of your voice, is a talent that makes you an all-time leader.

  The ones with high-pitched tones are seen as less empathetic, more argumentative, annoying and ruling. But at the same time, people with lower pitches are seen as less confident and more nervous kind of speakers, even if they're not. This perceiving is a basic human quality and you can't care less about it. All you can do, it to focus on how and when to vary and modulate your tone.

  Pitch is the rate of vibration or the frequency of the sound wave. Voice modulation helps to make use of all the three parameters and blend them to make an adorable voice. Pausing while talking for less than 2 seconds can help you gather your thoughts before talking again. This way, you won't stumble and your speech is going to get even better.

  It is also smarter to read and scan the room, you'll be talking in. The people, echo, audience, and the topic in specific. The more you are aware about the external factors, the more your speech is going to get better. Although we are discussing about non-verbal communication here, the preparation needed right before you speak, and while you speak is as quintessential as your speech.

- **Effective communication** – Effective communication puts light on how effective of a leader you are. The one that can talk and influence has been seen winning the world. It is not about the wide vocabulary you have, it is about how effectively you deliver your thoughts. Leaders are the ones who motivate, empower and push the bar way high for the employees to deliver their best. Hence, making communication skills an important non-technical skill.

- **Emotional Intelligence** – It can basically be seen as the ability to understand the right amount of 'emotional quotient' you express and receive from others. There are various aspects as to control one's emotional intelligence, just like intelligence quotient.

- **Avoid Fidgeting** – Playing with your hair, rubbing your eyes and/or ears, checking phone constantly, adjusting your jewellery and getting distracted by literally everything can point at your low interest levels and add up as your lower capability to be more attentive.

Pay attention to your breathing: take deeper breaths and avoid short, hasty breaths. Monitor your body's movements: if you fidget too much, be aware of the root cause and try to relax. Letting go of your own tension allows you to pay more attention to the person talking and also on what you got to talk.

Put away your distractions, like your phone and try calibrating your energy levels with the ones you're in a room with. Being emotionally aware of when and how to react, on what terms, and how much to react is also a technique in itself that has to be inculcated.

When we're nervous or stressed, we all pacify with some form of self-touching, nonverbal behaviour as mentioned previously like adjusting your hair, dress and jewellery automatically makes you an overly self-aware person, which might not be the impression you want to give away to your work environment.

If you catch yourself indulging in any of these activities of fidgeting, take a deep breath and steady yourself by placing your feet firmly on the floor and your hands palm down in your lap, on the desk or on the conference table. Stillness sends a message that you're calm and confident.

Fidgeting has always impacted adversely on the individual's abilities to function productively. Although a very small portion of body language, this overall sums up to be the most important part of mastering your body language. You just have to start observing your patterns or start asking someone to do it on your behalf, so you can just work on the parts where you lack.

To sum it all up, there are certain things that are gender-specific as discussed in all the above points, but at the same time applies equally to every individual working in corporates. Although there are certain things to keep in mind if you are a working woman and an aspiring leader at any given organization, before discussing further.

- **Things to avoid while stressing on Body language** (*For women*) –

1. **Do not** use too many head tilts, especially being a woman, you have to understand the difference between acceptance, and submission. A woman is by default expected to adjust to every scenario and decision. If you aren't happy with something, display it confidently on your face. Express disagreement and nodding too much ***DOES NOT*** make you a better leader.

2. **Do not** give away your power, as it is rooted deep, for women to be submissive. The solution to this is to be strategic when you smile. When making an important business point, think through if smiling will help you in your situation or not. You ***DO NOT*** want people to take your point less seriously because you were smiling through it.

3. **Do not** condense yourself, by taking up as less space as you can. Take up larger room, with wide open arms, and free aura. Men often give away this idea of occupying larger space compared to women at workplace, making them a ever ready, confident leader.

4. **Do not** fall in your own trap of being too girly, giving out the similar features, like adjusting your hair, jewellery, and dress. Avoid wearing anything flashy, or something that would require extra attention from you while working.

5. **Do not** back off or contain yourself from talking and making your point. Women are always seen waiting till the last moment, to talk and ask questions. It although isn't a bad habit to wait around for someone to finish, but know when to talk, and make sure your tone is authoritative and assertive enough.

6. **Do not** smile excessively, for women smiling often is misinterpreted as trying to be flirtatious while making a strong point, or in a serious conversation. Whereas smile can be the most powerful tool during your first impression and can be seen as confidence on your face, but if done overly, it is often misinterpreted.

7. **Do not** be overly emotional and expressive while showing your happiness or disagreements. When you appear calm and contained, you look more powerful. Women who visibly express their emotions with hand gestures that rise above their shoulders can quickly overwhelm an audience, especially when it's an institution full of men.

8. **Do not** forget how important perfect and firm handshakes are. A woman with weaker handshakes are often seen as unconfident and less worthy of the position they're being offered. Take the time to cultivate your "professional shake." Keep your body squared off to the other person, facing him or her fully.

----

CHAPTER 5

8 Leadership Styles – How To Find Your Own Style

L eadership in its basic definition summarizes to constantly motivate, guide and look out for those who are always heading ahead, knowing their leader has got their back. Power of a leader lies in his/her employees/coworkers confidence. A corporate leader is said to have won, if even one of his employee faces any difficulty at work, with most efficacy and feels confident and is looking for ways to progress.

It is always said that "Power is not in dominating your fellow employees, but to strengthen their roots in workplace effectively." In all the circumstances, a good leadership is considered a way towards successful business growth. A leader's substantial role is to help the employees understand their weaknesses, strengths and inputs to work. It is a vital thing to coincide the work intentions with that of the personal goals. Being an effective leader, you show them what it is to face the challenges, bravely, just like you had to do, when it was your time.

Humans function differently and with a whole different set of instructions while handling work. Carrying out leadership is as hard and challenging as it seems like. Doing it effortlessly is a definitive form of art. There have been researches and studies that were carried out over the time and hence it has been laid down that there are different types of leadership styles that have been proven efficacious in the past.

Finding the right leadership style is a stretching and difficult job to do. But once you've discovered, the results are going to be fruitful. "Understanding how you lead and want to lead will give you a better sense of control over the size and scope of your reach and impact", says plains Joyel Crawford, a leadership development consultant.

Leadership styles are often drawn back from your personalities, preferences, and background. Knowing which one works natural for themselves is one of the most satisfying feelings. Being able to switch between various leadership styles considering the quality and quantity of work is also quintessential.

Here is a detailed research on different effective leaderships and how they would suit different people with multiple personas –

- **Autocratic Leadership** – Establishing end to end goals, divisive work, setting up of guidelines for what, how and when the goals need to be achieved, is all about an Autocratic leadership. It is also referred to as an Authoritarian leadership. This leadership is considered to be one of the most effective leaderships during a shorter time to finish the work.

  This type of leadership is a naturally laid down, fully planned and systematically arranged one. The autocratic leaders expect the instructions to be followed right on time The focus of Autocratic leaders is to effectively get the work done through established actions keeping in mind the company's best interests. The autocratic leaders are not always the one who knows it all, they just tend to follow a certain protocol to work systematically.

  Results are dominantly visible in corporate zone. No leader can just be categorized into being just good or bad. It is just the difference in the way of handling everything. In autocratic leadership style, the employees look out for clearer guidance and instructions as to how to carry out the work assigned and meet the deadline effectively. It is often implemented when there is little time for putting for the detailed plan.

  An adequate leader will know precisely on how to get his/her peers into confidence in case the work requires the change in work schedule, acceptance of guidelines. In autocratic leadership, one thing has to be given special attention, which is to give clearer guidelines. In case of failure of guidelines, the work will fall clinging and incomplete.

You know that you master at this leadership type, if you are a great decision maker, rapid planner, and someone who doesn't put themselves above their peers. You keep it simple and act on little things that will effectively help you reach you and your team mates to the desired goal.

"A leader is one who knows the way, goes the way, and shows the way" – John C Maxwell.

- **Pacesetting Leadership** – Working on pressure, meeting the deadlines, keeping the duration small and tight is the highlight of this type of leadership. The leaders keep it uptight on their guidelines, instructions and team. Goal is to run hard and reach the finish line, no matter what the hurdles are.

It is by default expected out of employees to function a little more, hard and extra than the usual in Pacesetting leadership. The leader gets to get on stronger and imposing the immediate functioning of his/her instructions. Pacesetting leaders are highly energetic, dynamic and zestful in the accomplishment process towards the goal.

The corporate units with production, and manufacturing environment. It is expected out of employees working under a pacesetting leader, to roll up their sleeves and jump into the task completion. This type of leadership works wonders when the company, leader and employees' interests and energies match.

Although it comes with greater risks of mental and physical stress in the employees. While it requires extra work and shorter span for meeting deadlines, but has been proven effective in some organisations to indulge in certain amount of pressure, that's going to keep you busy and engrossed. It is one of the most crucial leadership, especially when you are wanting to meet short-term deadline. It requires highly-motivated employees to function under this type of leadership. The results unlike most times can be witnessed quickly here.

This type of leadership has a high chance of employee burnout, if the employees are constantly expected to function 100%.

Dynamic energy under the guidance of pacesetting leaders can be engaging for employees who thrive in a fast-paced workplace. Detecting mistakes although gets strenuous and burdensome in pacesetting leaderships.

If you are a leader who likes to start and finish early with utmost pressure, hard work and boss around to get the work done, then you know your natural way of leadership is pacesetting.

- **Transformational Leadership** – Long term goals, elongated observations, and structural inputs to set the future goals better, is the best definition of transformational leadership. The transformational leaders work intensely for the betterment and growth of an organization. Most growth-minded companies tend to adopt this kind of a leadership style.

They truly set up a whole goal of futuristic ideas to be achieved and hence motivate and push the employees onto focusing on reaching there mutually. In this type, the deep-rooted inputs given in by the employees are taken into consideration and then a detailed report on how the organization can have better growth goals.

Setting objectives and mapping out on where the company has to reach and how the goals of growth can be acquired by motivating and inspiring the employees to innovate. Transformational leadership is most effective in fast-growing organizations or organizations that have been drifting and need direction.

Transformational leadership enhances the future vision of the company by setting the goals with futuristic development. This is observed to be a rather slow process and a development that can be negligibly observed due to it being a slow process. Under transformational leaders, people have tons of autonomy, as well as plenty of breathing room to innovate and think outside the box.

It is highly anticipated out of transformational leaders to boost employee morale and retention if workers feel genuinely connected to company goals. One major con of this type of leadership is that, when the linchpin is the bigger goals, smaller milestones get missed out on the way. Present day issues may be sacrificed for long term goals. Leaders are able to establish a high level of trust with employees and rally them around a shared vision or end goal.

Although, in environments where existing processes are valued, this desire to change things up can ruffle some feathers.

So, if you are someone with a gut of imagining the future with better opportunities, goals and intentions for the company, which in turn pulls you into being a leader, with greater goals, then you know you are a transformational leader.

- **Coaching Leadership** – Individual focus and growth, tapping individual strengths and building the organizations with the whole of team is the kind of coaching leadership. This is a form wherein you as a coaching leader, become a constant support system for the employees to lean on and ask help from. This predefines and figures out the strengths, weaknesses of individuals in the company and pushes them to perform their 100%

This style focusses basically on mutual growth of employees and the organization. As a coach-style leader, one looks up at their team as a reservoir full of untapped talent and resource. Their opinions, views, and feedbacks are constantly taken into consideration for improving in the future.

Coaches give the employees constant feedback on what and why they are lacking in certain areas of work, and nurture the individual in a slow process, just so he/she in turn can be an asset to the organization. Leaders from this type constantly provide challenging situations, to figure out the weaknesses and strengths of individuals.

This is also a long term leadership goal similar to that of the transformational leadership; the difference is that coach-style leadership purely pivots on the growth of individual, whereas transformational focusses on growth of the organization only.

'This leadership style denotes the importance of the betterment of employees, and not just the organizational growth.'

Coaching leadership is most effective when leaders have the time to devote to individual employees and work on the larger good than just the organizational growth. This style works best with employees who know their limitations and are open to changes and challenges.

This leadership highly promotes skill development by helping the individuals indulge in their own betterments. This promotes for a naturally pleasant learning environment which doesn't make anyone feel weaker or stronger. This also promotes equality and unity among the employees.

- **Democratic Leadership** – The word 'Democratic', talks for itself… It basically involves a leadership, wherein the opinions of his/her fellow employees, matters. The inputs from the employees are taken extensively before a leader makes an exclusive decision for the organization's benefits.

  A regular course of dialogue, discussion, debates, arguments and opinions are put forth the entire team to resolve a problem or situation that arose. A democratic leader ensures that the decision taken is with respect to the innumerable opinions. Although, the final decision still lies with the leader himself. This mostly reduces the chances of the meeting failures and loses, since the possible negative impacts have been discussed and addressed.

  Democratic leadership, also called as participative leadership is the type where the participation of every individual is crucial, it promotes diversity in the decision. This type of leadership is highly motivating and powerful in situations wherein there's plenty of time to plan, process and execute things. In matters requiring high creativity and inspiration, this leadership is proven to be effective. They aren't handing down orders from on high, and instead take a much more collaborative approach to getting things done.

The best part of this leadership type is that, every employee in that respective team would feel heard and his opinions would get a platform for showcasing the skills, he/she masters at. This can turn super-effective when the employees have immense trust on the one leading their team. This helps build the sense of co-working in a safe and voiceable environment. Creativity and innovation are encouraged, which also improves job satisfaction among employees and team members.

These democratic leaders work for the benefit of both the employees and the organization. The goal will be simply to achieve the growth and meeting of deadlines. But in a way that wouldn't harm neither of the participants.

Democratic leadership fails if you are constantly trying to achieve consensus among a group. It can be inefficient and, in some cases, costly.

If you are a leader, who thinks the best meetings are the ones where everyone has an equal chance to weigh in and if you can't remember the last time you made an important decision without getting input from at least one other person, then you know you are a democratic leader.

- **Affiliative Leadership** - Collective decision making, top priority – employee well-being, are the things that makes up the affiliative leadership one of a kind. The goal in here is to put employees first, by meeting their emotional and professional needs. This promotes harmony, peace and consistency in the decision making process.

Affiliative leadership also called as the facilitative leadership, tells how crucial it is for the employees to have a common say when it comes to decision making in a team. It establishes collaborative relationships within the teams.

Ultimately, the decision making still lies with the leader, but during the entire process, the team is allowed to completely explore the negatives, positives and possible outcomes. The affiliative leaders use praise as the major tool and weapon to instigate the sense of confidence and motivation among the teammates.

This type of leadership is most effective when there is a wide difference in opinions and the morale is very low among the inmates. It can also be helpful during the times of high stress during short-staffed or a busy season. These leaders are expected to aggressively be able to solve higher-level conflicts leading to the disruption of the organization's harmony.

Affiliative leaders make the lives of employees a little less complicated by prioritizing the well-being of their professional and personal lives. Their workplace enthusiasm is expected go up an extra notch. This enhances the chances of resolving a conflict in a far better way.

If you are really somebody who understands the hurdles in maintaining the work-life balance, and hence you make your employees life a little better, and you take their emotional topics into consideration and not be rude while listening to their problems, then you know you are an affiliative leader.

- **Delegative Leadership** – Minimum Guidance, minimalist involvement of leader, workspace filled with loads of learning, is the type of Delegative leadership. It is also called the 'Laissez-faire' as the leaders provide minimum guidance for carrying out certain amount of work. This allows the team members to distribute the responsibilities among themselves and carry out the work with utmost efficacy.

'Laissez-faire', is a French term that translates to "leave it be," which pretty accurately summarizes this hands-off leadership approach. It's the exact opposite of micromanagement. Laissez-faire leaders provide the necessary tools and resources. But then they step back and let their team members make decisions, solve problems, and get their work accomplished—without having to worry about the leader obsessively supervising their every move.

The level of trust and freedom that an employee receives from a leader is considered highly motivating and empowering. This creates a sense of free-will to work and promotes lesser interference and monitoring by the supervisors/leaders.

Delegative leadership is most effective when employees are highly qualified self-starters with strong track records. . It's also useful in situations when trusted employees engage in individual projects or when creative tasks or problems require out-of-the-box thinking.

Delegation of work among the employees will help the leader focus on major other issues that need to be handled by someone more eligible and qualified like the leader himself. This type of leadership will help boost the confidence of the employees who have had good experiences and competence.

While this leadership style can empower, it may also limit development, therefore, must be kept in check. This will require a detailed set of instructions to help delegate the power and structured functioning system. Due to absence of constant supervision, this can bring out indifferences amongst the employees and hurt the morale of the organization and this in turn can deteriorate the personal status of an individual employee.

If you, hardly do any of the talking in project status update meetings. Instead, your team members are the ones filling you in on where things are, and you're really only involved in most tasks and projects at two key points: the beginning and the end, then you know you are a Delegative leader.

- **Servant Leadership** – Inclusion of morale values in decision making, not bossing around, and collective responses sum up for the servant leadership. These leaders exhibit the importance of handing over the disciplinary of making decisions in an organization to the employees/ team members.

Servant leaders among many other type of leaders, share power and decision-making with their subordinates and often direct the organization based on the team's interests. Servant leaders operate with this standard motto: Serve first and lead second.

Despite the fact that they're natural leaders, those who follow the servant leadership model don't try to maintain a white-knuckle grasp on their own status or power. Instead, they focus on elevating and developing the people who follow them. Their wellness is their top-most priority.

"Leaders are the ones who are willing to give up something of their own for us. Their time, their energy, their money, maybe even the food off their plate. When it matters, leaders choose to eat last," says Simon Sinek.

This leadership style can be effective for all organizations and teams that need to create diversity, inclusion and morale. This leadership boosts morale and leads to a high level of trust, hope and promising nature which results in better employee performance and a more positive company culture overall.

Although it comes with a challenge of constantly pushing your own needs and priorities to the backburner isn't something that comes as second nature for most of us.

You Might Be a Servant Leader If… You're known for asking, "What can I do to help?" at least three times a day and you place a high priority on removing roadblocks and helping others get things done, you never think twice about helping out when you're asked—because you know that your own to-do list will still be there when you return.

- **Why is it important to know your leadership style?**

  Leadership isn't something that cannot be untapped and brought into existence. I believe we are all born leaders and knowing what is the natural way of our leadership style. It motivates an individual and builds the confidence to know that they haven't been doing anything wrong, they've just been doing it differently.

  "There's a whole lot of difference in doing things wrong and different."

Now that we understand the nitty-gritty of leadership, different leadership styles, and other aspects, it is important to understand why you must know what does suit you the most? Which leadership style brings out the best in you? Answers to these will help you understand things a lot better.

It is the basic human character to familiarize yourself with the ins and outs of the above approaches…what if you've realized that you want to make some changes? Perhaps you've pegged yourself as a transactional leader and want to be more transformational, or you think you could incorporate more servant leadership into your existing style.

Knowing that leadership is a whole process of learning and it being a longer one, it takes lots of trials and errors to figure out your natural way of leadership. Regardless of the efforts, one should always feel comfortable and flexible to be able to shift between different types of leaderships. And this is possible only when you have heard your natural instinct speaking out loud on what your leadership style is.

That's when the idea of 'Situational leadership', comes into picture that a leader can shift from these different types and can be great at doing so. Knowing your leadership style also helps you decide which organizations might be a better cultural fit.

It's important that you maintain transparency about what you're focused on as a leader, and to help create alignment around your vision and objectives, it's important to create a culture where people understand the strengths that they collectively bring to the team.

The wisdom of figuring out which is your leadership style, will make you a stronger, trust-worthy, and reliable leader of all times. It helps you understand your team well. In the end, leadership is all about, accepting the diversities of employees and the asset building they do with the organization.

CHAPTER 6

Process Of Women Being Stronger Leaders In Workplace

No matter for how many decades we debate the ongoing gender inequality and the mistreatments of women at workplace, this have consistently sustained over the years and has gotten its roots deep within. Women have always showcased that being a leader, is a thing they can excel in. But the immediate factors like office politics, gender based inequality, and a sense of incapability drives a woman's confidence to ground zero.

Empowering yourself being a woman, whilst you empower other pack of women who look up to you, or are dependent on you, will change the whole narrative. As we better understand and make the critical connections between gender and social equity, it's time we take action towards solutions.

The process of becoming a leader is far more challenging than handling the whole set of responsibilities of a leader itself. It's always the struggles, weaknesses, obstacles, and small-scale wins that defines your journey of becoming a successful leader.

Not everyone's success stories are the same, but trust me, everyone's story is always quite worth listening. Because, you learn from the mistakes other's committed while climbing the same ladder, you plan of climbing in next 15 years. Also explicitly if you're a woman, the struggles are going to another extra mile high.

Practicing resilience, having humility, playing to your strengths, taking risks, helping others, and finding mentors are the key to becoming an effective woman leader. Do not let anyone tell you that you are weak, or incapable of doing and achieving something in life. Corporate success comes with consistency, hard work and constant small unnoticeable wins. Make sure you make it worth your while.

Here are a few important processes that will help you become an effective leader –

- **Fight for Mindset of Equality as Reality** – Women have a considerably less pay than most men. A study conducted by the Pew Research Center found that in 2020, women earned 84% of what men earned based on an analysis of the median hourly wage for both part-time and full-time work. Similarly, a 2020 U.S. Census Bureau study that analyzed full-time wage data found that women earned 83% of what men earned.

  Staying optimistic and motivated even when the inequality at workplace has surpassed all the levels of bearing, can definitely be helpful in a way. Pretending like everything is normal and that there's progression even when there isn't, can make it look like the gap never existed. Paula Stephenson, director of marketing at Smoke's Poutinerie, says if women want to be viewed as equal in the workplace, they must stand their ground and demand the respect they deserve – and it starts by behaving as if the gap has been closed.

  If you act like there's equality in the workplace, then there will be.

  Facing gender gap in every woman's career, is a breakthrough into the topic of how unequally, the system works. The corporate offices have although improvised a lot in order for the inequality to start perish. Some are even proven to be effective.

  A pay dispute, a lost promotion or snide comments from co-workers, it is literally everywhere. Even if your work environment excels at providing a safe equality, it's not uncommon to encounter people who have faced some kind of discrimination, subtle or not, because of their gender.

  Working mothers especially walk on the fence and take up all the inequality burden of handling work, whilst they breastfeed and nourish their new-born. A strong woman leader in you, will never give up on a person suffering discrimination based on gender or anything for that matter.

Facing the discrimination, inequality and gender gap is on one side, acting out against is another way of handling it. Remember that if you choose to bear with it, someone else will do it too. If you decide and fight it out, you benefit a larger suffering community. Be that leader and inspiration to thousands of people.

- **Women embracing their Natural Leadership style** – We all have different sets of weaknesses and strengths. Some find solace in helping others grow, some have a distinct methodology of solving a problem. Finding out the leadership style that truly keeps you going, and yet addresses the problem-in-picture, is very crucial in becoming a constructive and efficacious leader.

  Be an open, supportive, and optimistic workforce in yourself. When someone new enters your work place, make sure you make it a safe place for them. Be a mentor, a friend and the first person they would want to go to, when they're having a rough day. Women can help others set goals and attain them, emphasize teamwork, and invest time in training, mentoring and personal development.

  Leadership isn't always about imposing and insisting authority and power of the ones below you, its about you looking out for them when they need you. When the problem surfaces, how you handle it all together as a team is what makes an effective leader. In the previous chapter, as we discussed leadership styles and about what and how it can affect you is crucial.

  As people work toward gender equality in their workplaces, the gender gap will close over time. Companies have a better chance of thriving when they incorporate various leadership styles, including what's seen as traditionally feminine or masculine.

- **Engage in Honest Open Communication** – Communication between an employee and a leader is like a door to progress, it emphasizes the level of comfort and safe space you develop with your coworkers. The company you're running and are responsible for, is the clear water reflection of your ethics, the transparent communication protocol you've set up.

The honesty and transparency should be the highest priority for any leader leading a pack of skilled minds. The importance of open and honest communication remains underrated in corporate. Your team follows the ethical values set up by you as a leader. So make sure you lead by an example. Make sure to convey the rules, follow ups, and task assignments the organized way, like you want it to be.

A leader who is good at communicating his feelings and intentions out, is the one you'll always see on top because of all the entitled good teamwork that has been carried out.

"Conveyance of your thoughts is an art which can be inculcated by every leader."

Avoidance of the friction caused between the employees and the leader, caused by poor or no communication, can do wonders in helping your company rise to heights. This also proves that any team takes a short while to function and wrap a task, in turn increasing the efficacy of the leader herself.

Communication improves to build the trust, develops a bond between the employees, enhanced active listening, defines clarity, improvises to ask open-ended questions, routes transparency, and helps receive and implement feedback.

When communicating with employees, speak in specifics. Define the desired result of a project or strategic initiative and be clear about what you want to see achieved by the end of each milestone. If goals aren't being met, try simplifying your message further or ask how you can provide additional clarity or help.

An honest open communication is powerfully collaborative with increased efficiency and encouraged positive engagement at work.

- **Grow connections with your team** – While we talk about how important communication is with your team members, it is very crucial to not miss out on how important it is for you, as a leader to develop the empathetic and professional bond with your teammates.

Women leaders master at the skill of seeing through the person, may it be an employee, a team member or even someone from the hierarchy above. Being empathetic with someone who's potentially going to serve their best for your company, is truly an asset for a longer time.

The mutually shared connection with your team member defines the trust they've developed over the time. The culture of accountability and exceptionally brilliant performances are showcased in an environment where the shared trust is a priority. With that culture in place, the team can achieve a successful business, a happy team and a fulfilled leader.

Empathy is believed to be the top leadership skill needed to successfully execute several corporate business functions. Therefore, leaders must acknowledge and be empathetic towards the perils and adversities their employees face. If need be, they should put themselves in employees' shoes and make decisions that benefit them.

Having discussed about how vital connecting and communicating with your team member is, it is also quintessential to know what the boundary of personal and professionalism is. There's a thing called personal and publicly hid information. Try and not wreck the relationship by stamping that boundary. Also it is important to acknowledge that we all have different ways of functioning and try and get an insight into their goals and motivations, which will help you, as a leader to perform better.

- **Vitalize Professional and Personal Growth** – A true leader will understand the importance of cultivating the behavior of maintaining the professional and personal life balance. Growth is an element of success and a leader rightly figures what is the necessity of growing personally while they help grow the company they're representing.

Especially for a woman leader, the growth almost feels stagnant considering their personal life progress of putting up with work culture discrimination, inequality and gender based pay bias. When a woman enters her pregnancy phase, the company no matter how big of an asset she is, she will still be seen as a liability. It is important to acknowledge and respect the fact that she needs that mental calmness and stability in life for her to also grow as a person whilst your company grows alongside.

In contrast to men, who tend to be career-centric and want to maximize their financial return from work, women view work more holistically, as a component of their overall life plan. Having said what it takes for both the genders, it is essential to note that this isn't a fight. It clearly is a demand for rights.

Investing in your employee's personal growth goals in the next 5-10 years and what they're expecting out of you (a leader and their mentor) is crucial to know and address. Their emotional side will indirectly affect their performance in your company, do not oversee and ignore it. Try and address their issues, in order to help them and your company grow.

Having to become a person that your team is going to look up at and reach out when they encircle themselves in problems is an incredible way to develop the emotional bond between you all.

Indulge in scraping out the creativity and talents from among your team members. Assign them with various tasks and get the productivity. Learn to inspire and motivate your team members

Leadership strategy is about empowering others to do their best and take on new challenges. A great leader will empower their employees to grow by giving them challenging opportunities and guiding them as needed, but at the same time will give them freedom on making decision and choices.

Understanding the fact that the company's growth lies in accordance with the individual's growth is the key to numerous tremendous success.

- **Maintain Optimistic Attitude** – Obstacles in a company's operations do not come all announced with big notice. They always come when you're running out of time and you're least expecting it to pop up out of nowhere. In times like this, a leader makes up his army in a way that the problem can be tackled with utmost efficiency, energy, and peace.

  Staying and maintain the calm when there's an internal storm subsiding is an intelligent and careful move. This way you put up an attitude of positivity that shines through you to your employees. Learn how to deal with negative implications of the unforeseen circumstances knocking at your doorsteps.

  Wearing a positive attitude right on your sleeve, rebuilds your employees' and teammates' trust on you. Not always they're going to be all inspired and motivated, at times like that, you as a leader have to lead them by telling how problems and negative impacts are meant to be overcome quoting from your past experiences and by staying positive.

  "Look at three positive things about a problem before you identify what makes it dissatisfying. The more you look at the positives in a problem, the more positively people react with one another." - Robert Mann, author of The Measure of a Leader (iUniverse, 2013)

  It is proven that a positive workplace environment is more likely to increase employee production and positive engagement by displaying enthusiasm and confidence, a good leader will see the impact that they can have in their working environment

- **Mentor employees instead of dumping orders** – Speaking of creating a collaborative and extensive work environment, the difference between coaching and controlling has be understood well. The leaders will focus completely on how to coach the employees emotionally, mentally and physically rather than burdening them with unethical bossing.

  It is quintessential to acknowledge the efforts an employee is putting in for the company. It is wide evident from my previous experiences that the employees function a little more productively knowing their work culture is friendly and their superiors are of friendly behavior.

Controlling the pack according to the way you want things to happen, will root out the entire company's integrity because, there are people who will function differently, yet productively, in turn reaching the goal. So as a leader you need to understand and acknowledge how this hierarchy of assignment of work functions.

Diversity in the way people think, function, and perform are quite different. As a leader, one needs to understand that the employees are in search and need of your constant support and you ordering and imposing instructions on them will only deter their productivity.

Especially for women leaders, it is important to feel how nearly impossible it gets to function in a bossy environment. So create a space where everyone looks out for constant mentoring and not be another product of getting orders from superiors.

People wouldn't grow if leaders never taught them anything. Leaders need to be teaching so they can grow new leaders to take their place.

- **Set Clear Employee goals and Expectations** – Understanding the clarity of small term and long term goals and setting up an elaborated instructions on how to reach the expected destined successes. Employees play a very vital role in reaching the goals, encourage questions and feedback, include them in the process and increase engagement.

It is merely a myth to assume that progresses and successes comes with just one person's implementation of ideas. In reality, only the effort put together by an entire team will surface success. It is important for you as a leader to showcase and preach your ideas, expectations and goals to your employee team members.

Working all together, with an intention of reaching the same destination, is when you embrace success and climb up the ladder.

Regardless of seniority level, every employee should be able to articulate how the work they do supports the success of the company and yet promotes self-growth.

Constant revisiting of the goals of both long term and short term and the openness to modification of the goals and reassuring them over the period of time is vital for company's growth. An effective leader will always make sure that the goals and expectations are announced out loud and that it should align with the employee goals as well.

"When goals are clearly set, everyone can track progress and identify achievements in a tangible manner."

- **Handout Feedbacks on Employee Performances** – Figuring out where and how your team is performing is the first thing, troubleshooting the places where your team is headed low and giving them the honest, open and genuine feedback so you all could head towards the company goals together is the foremost important thing.

As a leader, make sure you observe the drawbacks and uplifted characteristics of your team members. Allocate a day in a month, quarter, or a year and talk about where your team is doing great and in which field they're lacking. Guide them constantly in overcoming if they're lacking in a particular subject. Help them to develop the nature of accepting criticisms and turning it into progress.

Criticism is the key to climbing the success ladder faster. Women leaders must emphasize on how subtly the criticism can be conveyed. Considering how sensitively employees might react and how adversely it might hurt you coworkers' ego is crucial.

Know the difference between being rude and conveying the feedback. Make sure the company's goals are being met along with the employees' personal growth, while addressing the feedbacks given by their leaders is progressive, subtle, and meaningful.

"If you're not direct, people won't know what you truly think about them and their work, and they will never be able to improve. If you don't know the precise direction your company is headed, no matter how much you've communicated to your employees and leadership team regarding their individual performance, they will flounder when it comes to making decisions and taking actions".

- **Ask for your Feedback as a Leader** – As we discuss further on how one has to feel comfortable to take the feedbacks from their superiors and coworkers, it is you, as a leader's responsibility to gracefully take up the criticism and feedback occasionally on how your performance is, from your employees.

  Taking a criticism will only strengthen your leadership skill and will make you're a kind of leader to whom the opinions and feedbacks of his coworkers matter. The society has anyway portrayed a woman leader's image differently by making her look weak, emotionally uncontrollable and indecisive. Prove that women can be a lot more than what is beyond their expectations.

  Be calm-minded and open to the idea of taking a criticism and following up with it. Remember the goal is for you and your company to reach heights and not to just survive the economic wave. The drift is significant, and so is the employee feedback.

  Leadership coaching can also help you discover areas where you need improvement. A professional who helps you develop a plan to achieve your leadership goals can be more motivational than books and seminars alone. Be that mentor to others who're struggling to ace the leadership of their own.

  "You need time to integrate, process and reflect, and unless you go through those steps, you won't have sustainable change."

- **New Ideas are Lifelines: *Be Open to Them*** – Being Open to newer ideas from your team shows how wider of a panel full of ideas you respond to. Good leaders have the emotional intelligence to understand and accept that change is inevitable.

Instead of trying to maintain a status quo just for the sake of consistency, embrace change and innovation.

The emotional intelligence comes in various factors like Self-awareness, self-regulation, motivation, and social skills. The whole mindset of openness to newness is a drastic improvement in your emotional intelligence development.

Most experienced and smart leaders, when stuck in a place of confusions and uncertainty, think from another perspective. Having a panel full of experienced, fresher, field experts and sometimes even a clerk ends up solving the mountain-sized problem into a pea-sized one.

Be open to the idea of taking the opinions of people who thinks differently from you. It definitely is worth taking the risk, as the ultimatum is to arrive at the solution and to not juggle and reach backwards. Encourage discussions and debates on several issues that might surface in the near future, by not compromising on the time and urgency of the decision-making.

"When you're open to hearing the thoughts of the talent around you is when you truly embrace every possibility and potential, See things through till the end. Understand that there will be errors along the way, but if something doesn't work, try to figure out why and how before scrapping it."

- **Recognize your own motivation** – Every person working will know exactly what their reason, motivation, and purpose of their leadership is. It's just a matter of time before you sit and think about if you're in this to just make money or to bring up the change in the work culture that surely has treated you different.

Every leader comes across a phase where they realize that they're doing the leadership right when they intend to inspire people and how you're destined to make a difference, and you know it in your heart that you can do it and change people's lives for good. That's exactly when you should pat your back for being in the right track.

Knowing yourself and your motivation will help you build a diversified team full of people whose thinking and way of working differs from that of yours. You as a leader should realize that the path to success is when you are surrounded by differently thinking minds and not by the carbon copies of yourself.

Surround yourself with people who are not like you. As we have previously discussed there are multiple leadership styles, knowing which one you're currently practicing and how to switch between the different types of them, based on the situations, needs and urgency of the situation, is very essential.

Remember to keep yourself updated with the latest trend on how to be interactive with your team and how to achieve that emotional stability with your team. With hard work, dedication and strategic planning, you can lead your team to success. It is that when a woman succeeds as a leader.

CHAPTER 7

How To Boost Employee Engagement – Make Work Environment Fun

Workplaces today have proven to be far beyond from being just a place of work and more like your second home. You invest almost half of your productive time of the day working and confined to the one role you're assigned to do. This shows the graph of a human life drastically falling as the proverb goes, "ALL WORK AND NO PLAY MAKES JACK A DULL BOY."

Researchers have it that a happy employee is a productive employee. Employee engagement is one important and crucial thing to keep in mind for all the leaders out there. Engaged employees have a lot to offer you company, including their effort, hard work, ideas and time.

The main noticeable change that you will instill in your company by increasing the employee engagement is increased productivity, active involvement and better communication. Employees expect to feel invested, involved and responsible for the company's benefit. Making the work environment fun is a marvelous way of engaging better.

Being a women leader, it takes a little extra to organize your team and put things back to place and get the work done while maintaining the workplace fun. It is a tricky possession for a woman in leadership roles to function effectively and not give out a vibe of being slutty at workplace. Maintaining the right balance and conveying your intentions are purely professional is one tricky task. But pulling it off graciously is also a talent that can be developed over the time.

An engaged employee is enthusiastic about their work and actively involved in achieving the business's goals and interests that you all mutually manifest. They have a positive attitude about the organization and its values and are committed to their work. In contrast, a disengaged employee is someone who may be coasting through their work

It is essential to acknowledge that being an employee, you set up a strategy to monitor employee job satisfaction. As an employee, it has to be set clear that your job isn't just something that pays off your bill, but something you're happy with and take pride in while talking about it.

Engaged employees are committed to bettering their work and the company at large. They are unlikely to leave their position for a higher salary or better title at another company, which reduces your employee turnover rate.

Let's dig deep in and discuss other vital employee engagement ideas in detail –

- **Allocate Time for Fun** – As part of a corporate world, one should always understand how pressuring it is to be a part of it. The constant push to keep working without a break is surely not viable in long term for either the company or the employee. A leader will assert the right balance between taking fun breaks and working effectively.

  Machines and technology wouldn't have surfaced if human could work like them. It is logically a lot less to ask for in a tedious work environment. Encouraging employees and coworkers to engage in watching a sport that's airing live while being at office, Encouraging employees to talk about their funny encounters from the company over lunch or dinner, are a few fun work culture that employees would love to have.

  When I encourage workplace to be fun, I surely do not intend on making it a place where the work gets piled up during the fun time. Know your company well to understand enough on what is the lower pressure period in a month, or a year. Take your team out on dinner or order in their favorite Pizzas and show them that THEY MATTER.

  Most companies have already been having these team dinners and encouraging employee wellbeing. To acknowledge and adapt is the key to achieving your success.

While putting bean-sized efforts like this, you as a leader shouldn't oversee the long term benefit the company is going to have with increased employee engagement.

- **Offer Unique Employee discounts** – Talking of fun environment, who wouldn't love if your manager bought you free movie tickets? Knowing what your employees or teammates are into and are eager for, is a smart way of announcing discounts unique to their choices.

Host and set up a committee who would judge the employees or teammates based on their monthly performances on parameters like, active listening, constant new ideas, troubleshooting, problem solving, and a fast learner. Attract the employees and keep them keen on their monthly/weekly/yearly rewards for performing better.

Announce the latest most awaited movie tickets or tickets to a sport event screening or to watch over a football/cricket match in stadium. Make the offers as unique as the employee is. Most people might not even be interested in a football match screening, but might brighten their performance for a free shopping voucher from Nykaa. Know your employee.

These kind of activities will help motivate the employees into performing a little better every time and in turn will make themselves grow happily.

- **Vitalize Open Communication** – Establishing a sense of true space for open communication is never going bad. Not once throughout this book I have emphasized on how vital open communications are for rising up in a corporate ladder. Being a leader, you need to accept and learn that no good will come to you, if you fail to be an effective communicator.

Employee trusts builds up only when they have a sense of openness with their leader/ manager. It is not always about performance, work culture, or interest of work. It is about how satisfied your employee is from their job. You, being a leader should take up this as a primary concern for your success ladder.

When you engage in open honest communication, you manifest a safe space for the team members to adapt to. Effective communication in the workplace is an essential element of a business's progress. I personally believe that communication not only enhances employee engagement but also the overall effectiveness of a team. It also improves relationships. Communication assures that team members understand what they are working towards and why.

To keep up with the same level of progress towards employee engagement, make sure you send out employee engagement survey to understand the employee feedback better.

- **Use Value-based Employee Recognition** – The core values that every company embraces and that something every new employee looks up to hold in her/his future days, has to be implemented and reminded very often.

This makes it easier for the employee to know what they're working for and the ultimate goal to be achieved.

At times, the company oversees the values and whole set of principles on which the company was built. Bringing it back to action from just the papers will give your employees an added motive to be productive and 10x more interested.

Being a leader, help your coworkers and employees to connect with the company values as much as possible, which embodies the true sense of an urge to implement it. It embodies the essence with which you expect your employees to function.

- **Know your employees** – To rapidly grow and assert an environment of growth, you need to simply know what your employees really are. Knowing what interests them the most, what puts them down, what they struggle with, how they're juggling with their personal and professional life matters a lot.

It plainly shows that you being interested in knowing them better, has to directly do with their betterment along with your institution. The relationship you build with your work tribe is going to be very precious for you in the long go. Know your employees' aspirations, families, kids – their names, education and health issues.

Simply building a bond where one starts to feel comfortable opening up to you about their problems and aspirations will only prove beneficial to you as a leader. You need to exactly surround yourself with like-mindedness and with those who come from place which will push them into achieving greater good.

Trust me when I say, "While climbing the success ladder, you meet all the people you'd once met throughout your journey. Chose them wisely". The best and easy thing you can do is get to know your people, and have every manager get to know their people. As easy as it sounds.

- **Create Opportunities for Collaboration** – Workplace is a wide environment with multiple quintessential features deeply rooted in every employee. There has to be a door that's always open for innovation, newness and collaboration in a team.

It has been even previously noted that the employees with mere positive attitude and innovative nature are more drawn towards working more efficiently and be productive, since there's a large source of their interpersonal relationships.

Creating an environment filled with opportunities to collaborate and brainstorm on the ideas as unique as every employee will definitely increase the employee engagement overall. Getting to know each other's weaknesses, strengths and even productive time of the month will also render fruitful experiences in a company. A leader will help create an environment that's welcoming and safe. Be that leader for your team.

- **Elucidate on Employee Contribution** – When employees join an institute, they're more interested to be part of making vital decisions and not just be a dummy player in the organization. So, it is very crucial for you, as a leader to focus on talking more about how every employee contribution affects the entire organization. Even if it is negligible, it is vital to show their role in it.

If needed, draw a flowchart and a graphic on how seriously the roles of each employees are intertwined and interconnected. How largely it impacts the functioning of a company is everything an employee has to understand. So, the next time they're working, they're 2x more conscious on how they will impact the smallest of happenings.

It is indispensable to establish a criteria on how well and why they fit in the company. The aim overall should be to contribute collectively towards the betterment of the company while keeping in mind the morals and values.

Appreciate your best people in the team for performing greater than your expectations. Astounding participation and critical decisions deserve appreciation and recognition. Make your employees feel that their efforts matter and that they are truly making differences.

These kinds of appreciation will only push them into doing a lot better and you will benefit on a greater scale, as a leader. Lead them into a path of self-growth and development.

- **Prioritize work-life balance** – Finding the right balance between your personal and professional life can be a lot challenging than what a person from outside corporate can think of. We must have experienced it ourselves on how hard and unworthy it gets when you come home from a tiring day at work and you do not find someone to talk to. This can really be hard considering all the factors pressuring a person in her/his top career schedule.

Parents growing old and sick, fear of being left alone or single, pressure of new mothers, lack of recognition at workplace, fear of losing the current job, and burden of tackling time for family and work, can all be challenging to face at the same time.

Showing your people how and why they matter to you and your company, will help boost the employee engagement up by another level. Learn to encourage and bring in a model where the work hours are flexible, reasonable amount of paid time offs, flexibility is working model can all be a great way of showing they matter. Show them that you appreciate them and respect their time.

"Giving your employees a generous amount of PTO, longer lunch breaks or small gifts to show appreciation can all be helpful," said Omid Semino, founder and CEO of Diamond Mansion.

- **Offer Role Flexibility** – Lateral Mobility, is the most inexpensive and hassle-free way of keeping your employees engaged within your organization. Letting your employees switch teams and divisions laterally within the same organization, will expose them to a wide variety of operations to get a work done.

In most cases I have experienced, employees want a shift from the existing company to a whole differently modelled company. Although this seems tougher for a younger individual, but this will help them improvise their learnings while being equally productive for the organization they're working for.

Instead of letting them switch companies, you can simply offer a switch of teams and departments from within the company. This way, you do not end up losing your efficient employee and will still retain their wishes and choices of better learning opportunities.

Younger employees always have a tendency of looking forward to jumping in their career ladder. But they're still uncertain about different departmental roles and what truly interests them. Once you let them get exposed to different sets of departments, they will end up finding the department that keeps them motivated and challenged.

You, being a leader, should understand the true worries of your employees and should work in accordance to meet their concerns. Letting go of ego and closed behavior of a team, will rise the employee engagement well.

- **Maintain Transparency** – It is a proven fact that employees are prone to be more productive and adventurous in taking up work when they know exactly what's going on and why? It is one of the best ways of keeping your employees involved and informed.

  Being transparent is one greatest of decisions you will makes being a leader. This makes you a leader whose trust rests upon the employees of your company, making you a hero element and builds a sense of reliance on you. When you place your trust and be transparent about every major happening in the company, it makes your employees be highly motivated to work hard.

  Another vital step that can be taken is, by conducting occasional team meetings and gatherings to discuss and take individual opinions. This shows the employees that you value their inputs. It is even more beneficial if the employees are kept in the loop during the decision making process and not informing once everything is sorted.

  Building trust and offering transparency is the best investment you will be doing as part of engaging your employees. So do it right?

- **Offer wellness and growth opportunities** – As we discussed previously, the easiest ways to engage your employees is to offer them with wellness and progressive deals. Instead of offering them with a free cutlery set, you could simply offer them a company paid international work trip, or by offering a health insurance policy scheme for them and their family, or by making them aware of the policies that company offers for new mothers and parents when they need child care leave.

  Understanding your team, about what they're in need of and what they're seeking for, from workplace is very essential. Some younger employees will start considering their work bland since there's no new learning in the company. Make your team focus on how many opportunities they can end up having if they did some things differently. With minimal change in the role or their part, they can switch and explore different teams and departments and mentors.

This is why managers should keep a close eye on their team members and, as they continue their education or add to their skill sets, offer more responsibilities and opportunities.

Make them understand that there are numerous opportunities and choices within your company and under your mentorship. This anyway makes you a leader worth having and also keeps up with your constant employee engagement strategy.

- **Offer Coaching and Mentoring** – One of the crucial and quintessential things that makes you a remarkable and tremendous leader is when you are a great mentor and a guide. Employees always look out for that push they need to function a little extra. A pat on the shoulder when their ideas get approved by a corporate team.

Know that, the success of an employee, is a proof that you won at being a leader. Only a leader who has gone through the struggles without having a hand that always scrutinized their every move, will know how much of an extra mile they have achieved because of the push by their coach/mentor.

A true leader will know the value of being there for someone physically, mentally and emotionally. You never know what other people are struggling with in their personal lives. Instead of giving out the typical leader qualities of being egoistic and extremely arrogant, be the one your employees will turn to on random tea breaks to discuss about their problems and the hard hunt for solutions.

By connecting employees with others in the company who have expertise to share, you can open up pathways of communication and learning within the scope of your company. Mentoring can help employees do wonders by unlocking their innovative sides.

- **Provide multiple options for Feedback** – Not every employee behavior has to be the same, there are numerous ways that people deal with. There are introverts, ambiverts and extroverts. Having said this, it is obvious to know that not everyone is willing to be open about their feedbacks in public, which ends up being a dishonest review.

In cases like this, all that is expected from you, as a leader is to be patient, calm and understanding with your employees and to create an environment where they would feel safe and would want to fill out their honest feedback about a co-employee or a leader.

It could just be done by announcing anonymous feedback Saturdays, where the employees can fill out their forms of how and what needs to be changed or on how well or bad they like the culture of the workplace. In such cases, it is highly expected that cases of abuse and insults will also surface. Being a leader, know when and how to take up necessary actions. This will definitely keep your employees tightened to their seatbelts.

- **Make a point to integrate new hires** – This is a great and effective way of grabbing employee's complete attention right from the start. When a new employee joins a company, it is quite important to introduce comfort to her/him. Once they start feeling considered and involved, their engagement towards the company hits high automatically.

  It is important for an employee to be introduced to every single member of the team they're going to be in. The one on one interaction with the team will increase their chances of enjoying working in your team and by being mentored by you, as a leader. Being put out there in a place where the coworkers are welcoming and open, will definitely keep the new employees interested and pushed.

  Strong initial connections proves that your team works together and not individually, reducing the chances of feeling an outcast for a new hire. This should be like another family for any employee, where it feels safe to share their struggle stories, weakness and pain without being over-judged.

- **Develop a strong Company culture** – As important as other parameters are, enhancing your company culture is far more essential for building stronger engagement with employees. What company culture means? The google definition says, *"Company culture is how you do what you do in the workplace."* A good company will know how to follow, what they're pre aching on papers.

It isn't always about how well-structured and well-organized your company is, but it is about how well you, as a leader is imparting and impacting the ones working for you.

We shall understand this better by an example, if I am promoting a wellness brand, I support healthy employees in my workplace by installing a treadmill at workplace. If I am endorsing for a fresh produce supply chain brand, then I shall give 20% off on sitewide purchase for employees working in the company. This way, you're endorsing and believing and working on an idea which provoked you to start the company.

By doing this, you're giving out a strong image of your company to be promoting and practicing too. This makes your employees follow and preach the same on behalf of you. Developing a strong company culture is surely one easy way of engaging your employees.

- **Support Employee goals** – A leader should recognize the need to create an environment where discussing about individual employee goals does not seem like a crime. In most companies, the employees seem to not be comfortable to even discuss about their next 5 year plans, because of the fear of losing their current job.

Instead of inducing fear, hear out their struggles and goals to know their interest, aspiration and dedication. Create opportunities for their betterment, discuss their career goals openly, and find growth opportunities within their existing role or in a new position within the organization.

During working-from-home conditions, employers can schedule a one-on-one to discuss employees' goals and ways to grow, while narrating a story they're struggled through. This will make your employees believe that you're someone who will understand what they're talking about without brushing it off blandly.

- **Act On Feedbacks** – One major ways to increase employee engagement as we discussed previously is to get and give an honest feedback about their workplace, mentorship, abuses faced in their workplace and lack of growth opportunities.

An honest and real feedback will play a major role in deciding what you and company are. Taking up a negative feedback and turning that into a positive response from an employee who matter to the company, will proclaim how crucial it is to talk out loud. A great way to make employees feel engaged with the workplace is to show them you're listening by acting on their feedback.

Employees who are highly engaged with their job and workplace are around 17% more productive than non-engaged employees, since they enjoy their work and are committed to the overall goals of the company. Communicate what you're doing in response and why, as well as when employees can expect to see results of the changes.

- **Celebrate Milestones** – May it be a pea sized or a mountain sized victory, milestones are always meant to be celebrated and appreciated. Make sure you know how to divide the appreciation among all the employees that were part of it even from the lowest of levels. This increases employee engagement by 10x as they will be content and proud to be working for a leader who has words for appreciation.

It is considered as key to keeping up with morals and motivated employees. Milestones can be both personal and professional. Make sure you celebrate employees' birthdays, anniversaries or achievements in the company or in a different field elsewhere. Sending a personalized card or email on the company account or a mention in online team meetings. These are small things but are a great proven motivation-booster.

Appreciation come from the right squad will mean a lot to people. Know it, value it and respect it.

CHAPTER 8

Learn How To Adapt Remote And Hybrid Working In Organizations

The phenomenon of remote working was an almost alien term in a pre-COVID pandemic era, where going to the allocated workplaces and offices was considered the only right and available way to work. Remote working surfaced well during the COVID phase and since then has never become any less popular for working professionals.

Remote working has emerged as a savior for most of the employees across multiple companies. Initially, the idea of letting employees from home or anywhere other than traditional workplace was definitely a no-no. But lately all the companies believe in the idea of letting employees take the time away from workplace and yet being able to finish their routine tasks.

This obviously has proven to have additional pros rather than having cons. The greatest thanking is deserved by the telecommunication providing platforms and internet which has given the remote working a whole different meaning in itself. A decade ago, this entire thought of remote working and work from home was merely just an exceptional case or a situational emergency. The advancements in technology has enabled the employees and employers both to work effectively and efficiently from their own comfort.

The advancements are such that the companies are thriving with completely remote working teams. As long as the productivity is achieved, it doesn't matter much about who and from where the team is operating. The mass transition to remote working came about in the early stages of the COVID-19 pandemic. Beyond preventing illness from spreading – a sick team can't be as productive – remote work has proven beneficial in a number of ways.

The notion of collectives of workers gathering en masse to complete work together, for any reason other than waging war and treating illness and injury (usually caused by the waging of wars), didn't truly occur until the industrial revolution. Since, remote working is here to stay for long and good, we need to understand it better on how it is effective? How it has evolved? What the future has in store for employees and employers preferring work from home?

Let us understand effectiveness of remote working better in this section –

- **Work From Home; An easy answer to Increased Productivity** – With a known fact of having the modern comforts of home, beckoning employees' attention, it would've been completely understandable if the graph of productivity fell steep. But employers and company have seen a dramatic surge in productivity, considering employees are functioning stress-free and longer hours. The proven fact that we all are more comfortable at our homes, can even be utilized as a place for working since the transition from office desks to anywhere at home, has come a long way.

  This remote working has also enabled the employees to lead and maintain a happier and healthier lifestyle. The opportunity to have a work-life balance, is what remote working provides for. What's more productive than knowing your employees are thriving and that you are seeing progressive results as a leader?

  Studies have found that 40% of employees work more hours while at home, when compared to working in office. The data from the National Bureau of Economic Research shows these extended workdays are, on average, about 48.5 minutes longer. For full-time employees, this time could add up to more than 193 additional working hours in a year.

  Remote workers have a tendency to lead a reduced stressful life. A 2020 Nitro study also identified trends toward reduced workplace stress among remote workers. In that study, 29% of remote respondents said they were moderately stressed at work, down from 33% in 2019 when office work was the norm. The study also showed the number of employees who felt "extremely" stressed while working has declined. This figure fell from 17% in 2019 to 15% in 2020 as work shifted from in person to at home.

The Shift from Factories and Cubicles to Wi-Fi and Zoom, has significantly brought about a change from which going back seems like a crime.

Virtual employees are now capable of working whatever hours they please, from wherever they choose. Increasingly, flexible working options are becoming the top favorites, as companies seek to poach talent from competitors with old-fashioned and rigid policies. Enabling the employees to finally live a life with balance, health, and happiness.

The leaders in corporate need to understand this dramatic increase in the love for working from home rather than office and should facilitate and provide the employees to relish the benefits of work from home.

- **Improved Work-life balance; The best outcome of Remote Working**

The most satisfying and less appreciated outcome that remote working offers is the betterment in an employee's work-life balance. This is something very crucial and underrated. Employees are the happiest and productive when they-re having a balance between their private time and professional working hours.

While, we talk about the increased trends in work from home, it is obvious to assume that converting your home to office might become a major reason to stay disconnected with family, even when you're there. But the graphs and studies have shown the opposite. Employees feel more connected and involved in private chores when they're still working. Providing them with peace for having achieved the balance.

Researchers found that working from home improves work-life balance, increases productivity and fosters healthier lifestyles. It's a win-win situation that workers relish for its flexibility. According to the Ergotron's study, 75% of employees have achieved work-life balance since remote working emerged. The study also establishes that remote working employees have twice as much work-life balance as full-time office workers.

Fostering a positive work-life balance is a way to keep employees happy – and happier employees are more creative, work smarter and are more productive.

Being a leader, it is important to upgrade to a top-notch level and see the betterment remote working has to offer and about how to inversely profit your company by profiting your employees by making them avail the remote working module.

- **Eliminating Commute; Notable Benefit of opting Remote work** – Life without a commute has been the latest favorite mode of most employees since the COVID pandemic took over our lives. Although it seemed very problematic and new, we all genuinely have been happier to stay surrounded by our loved ones and work remotely from the comfort zones of our homes.

Commute takes up a good chunk of time from employees' life. A survey was conducted recently to understand how remote working has impacted the commuters. Among 1000 people, 31.4% are working from home due to COVID and 15% were working from home prior to COVID.

Those who are working remotely due to COVID, save an average of 49.6 minutes a day. This means that since the onset of COVID in mid-March, people have saved more than 4 days (4.13) from commuting, and for those who were already working remotely before COVID, they save on average 51 minutes a day by working remotely.

Commute does add up to become a very important offspring of remote working. Although, it isn't paid much attention to, it still is one major thing that people are grateful for. Reduced carbon footprints and benefitting the pockets of employees is another major attention to detail fact of lessened commute for work.

On an average, Indians spend 7% of their day in commuting to office, averaging less than 3 minutes per kilometer. Travel Time Report Q1 2019 report, is based on the data collated from the rides on MoveInSync platform across Bengaluru, Hyderabad, Chennai, Pune, Mumbai and Delhi-NCR.

The report found that office commuters in Chennai travelled the fastest at 25.7 km/hr, while Bengaluru and Mumbai commuters travelled the slowest, at an average speed of 18.7 and 18.5 km/hr.

Hyderabad and Delhi-NCR travelled at 21.2 and 20.6 km/hr respectively.

A significant number of employers lately have been understanding the need to provide a healthy and flexible working environment. And one of the best well-being initiatives to put in place is to bring about the remote working mode and offer a convenient way for the entire workforce.

- **Fosters Healthy lifestyle; Best benefit of adapting to Remote work** – It can go unnoticed completely when we miss out to address the invisible line between work and health. It is as important to listen carefully to your body, as it is for you to listen to your manager. Unhealthy lifestyle sometimes costs a lifetime of regrets in various forms. Remote work promotes and fosters the possibility for corporate employees to proceed with their busy work schedule and manage their health at the same time.

Some remote employees have found more time to build healthier exercise habits. According to researchers, 50% of remote employees take time to run or walk outdoors. About 35% of remote employees can now work out at home.

Leaders can help their remote team foster healthy habits by actively promoting teamwork with utmost self-care. The amount of energy spent on waking up, getting dressed and commuting to office and working the entire day, is rather frustrating and overwhelming for most employees and in this process, they tend to miss out on having physical exercise. The Remote work, came into the lives of employees as an unexpected solution.

Most of us try way too hard to manage and maintain the work-life balance. Leaders need to acknowledge the need for flexibility and fluidity. This fluidity can be achieved when you opt for remote work. It offers flexibility of work by letting you take breaks and spending time with your family, while you work.

Managers can be understanding and flexible when it comes to employees informing about needing a break during the day, for some personal reasons. It helps your employees embrace a well-sorted mental health. It won't put them in trouble to choose between family and work. It is important as a leader to allow the team to work around their schedules as work is always at their fingertips, and set healthy boundaries where work stops for the day or week.

Employers/ Leaders can help the employees/ coworkers to track their progress, goals and achievements. It pushes the employees to do an extra mile for the company when their well-being stands first for the company/ managers.

There are multiple ways, remote working is helpful. But most importantly, it is the best rooted solution to lead a healthy lifestyle.

- **Evolution of Remote Working** – Past ten years, remote working meant a lot many other things compared to what it is today. It has evolved dramatically and has spread its wings in almost all of the domains of work. It has emerged to be one of the best gifts that technology and science could have ever offered. I, personally come from an era where remote work, could not even exist in my head.

The time has evolved extraordinarily, where your colleagues had to take an extra mile to connect with you, if you were not at office, by sending you an email on your alternate Email ID, to immediately checking if you're online and sending a Microsoft Teams invite to discuss further. It also enables the employees to take the meetings from anywhere and at any time of the day.

We, Indians had to learn it the hard way that technology can be an accomplice instead of merely being a matter of national progress. Remote employment basically meant a telemarketing or customer service position at below minimum wage and couldn't be someone's full-time career. Now, the technology has evolved to a point where it enables the users to get the same job done no matter where you are, how far you are, and what time it is. You are provided with the ability to interact and work with multiple teams simultaneously working from different parts of the world.

Another best technological evolution that happened was video conferencing. The beautiful feature that enables the corporate teams to interact live and in real-time from any part of the world is extraordinary, which is next best thing to a face-to-face interaction. But this capability wouldn't be possible without the widespread broadband internet adoption of the past 10 to 15 years.

The advancement of technology in terms of remote working has made many companies celebrate a shift from traditional working spaces to remote working or co-working models. This rather saves up a lot of time to commute, rent payable for the office spaces and cumulative energy of all the employees.

Latest updates with respect to remote working is that people have started investing in setting up Co-working spaces, where employees from different domains and companies come together to work peacefully and remotely under a single roof. All they would need is access to internet. This was taken surprisingly well by all corporate employees.

The best of use for the remote working model came up when the world suffered a pandemic in 2019. When none of us could literally step outside for work or anything else for that matter. The evolution of internet adaptability needs to thank a big cluster of employees who found solace in working remotely and the ones who allowed for it.

- **Current State of Remote Working** – The drastic developments and advances the technology has to provide can never go unnoticed. Because of continuous internet access, remote working has become acceptable in most corporate offices. The model lately has been such that people prefer traveling while working, some turn up to nearby coffee shops with internet access, while some prefer staying at home and dealing with their career goals.

The teams with a modern workforce comprises of various types of employees whose working model is distinguishable from the other. The communication preferences varies too. The challenges that come up while working remotely can be a little stressful when compared to working physically with your team. This is seamlessly solved by continuous back-to-back meetings. Because by the end of the day, we're all somehow connected through the internet.

A report from 2023 survey exclaims that, most companies paid for expenses such as hardware, office equipment and supplies, with 64 percent of respondents indicating their company provided hardware and 40 percent reporting that items like a desk and chair were also offered. Internet service was given to 28 percent of remote employees.

While the desire and expectations of employees to work remotely keeps on increasing significantly every year, the companies are currently trying hard to bring about policy changes that could support the best interests of the employees.

A win-win situation can be proposed by taking off the office equipment investment (which significantly will be high) and instead replacing that with remote-working policies where the employees will have the authority to choose for their comfortable schedules. It embeds the feeling of freedom in employees to work from wherever they please.

- **Hybrid Working Model:** *An Emerging Solution* – This term called 'Hybrid working model', is something that emerged as a one-stop solution for all the corporate employees and as a savior for most companies. The obvious accelerated shift from traditional working model to remote and hybrid working model came mainly because of Covid-19 pandemic. As a result of which, most companies preferred keeping employees' choices above everything. That's when a term called Hybrid work model was introduced, that allows employees to work from home some days of the week and come into the office for the rest.

Some companies took a leap by extending the hybrid working model to permanence. Once the benefits of Hybrid model is learnt, most companies subsided with the effectiveness of the whole idea. Some companies who found solace in Hybrid model are; LTIMindtree, Google, Ford, Microsoft, Infosys, Wipro, Kantar, Shopify, TCS, Maruti and more.

As we settle into the post-pandemic world, companies are willing to adjust and continue working from home as the "new normal". Many companies have asked their employees to work from home as a permanent solution.

However, speaking of implementing the ethics surrounding the hybrid model in corporate workspaces, it is important to discuss it thoroughly with the employees and arrive at a joint decision by the management. Enforcing just because the management and upper level employees decided on it, seems more like a forced decision, which becomes ethically wrong at workplaces. It works the other way as well.

"We believe how we work is more important than where we work," said Facebook when it shared an update to its remote work policy.

- **Future and Remote Working** – As we discussed previously, the structured model of remote working is yet to be explored and discovered. But this remote working model is here to stay for long now. The better we welcome it with open arms, the better it will amalgamate with our futuristic concerns.

Remote options may continue to grow as technological advances such as AI are able to play a major role in managing remote staff. The organizations are on the verge to adapting remote working policies and capabilities, while some companies have already adapted it.

Putting in place, the standard key performance indicators (KPI), across all the departments of the company will help keep a track of performance and productivity of both management and employees. This way, the remote team members are aware of employee expectations, and about their performance being monitored. It's just like traditional in-office work, but from a distance.

This current model of remote-working might seem a little faulty, as many of the core questions and problems have not been addressed yet. But in the near future, this seems to be the most promising working model for the corporate employees. As more employees expect remote work options, more companies are investing in the tech and systems needed to support working from home.

With peace, stability, health, and money, remote working can simply be called as a one-stop solution for all the employees. It is very crucial that we start exploring and embracing the workplace innovation.

CHAPTER 9

How To Improve Your Work-Life Balance - Challenging But Crucial

Often we experience the imbalance between work and personal life struggles. And more often we tend to put work ahead of our private life. The desire to succeed professionally by making a career that is a dream for most set of people, comes with a cost of sacrificing your crucial young days with your spouse and parents.

Trying to find the right balance between the work and personal life, can be an adventure in itself, but worth giving a try always. Creating a peaceful and productive work-life integration is although burdensome and challenging, but it is very important for your emotional, mental, and physical well-being and is crucial for your career as well.

In brief, destruction of work-life balance happens due to lack of maintenance of equilibrium of choices between one's priorities over career and personal life. Sometimes it is caused by increased responsibilities at work, elongated long hours, burden of being new parents and increased responsibilities at home.

The pros of finding the balance are innumerable such as, relieved of stress, unexhausted, higher productive, energetic, and interested 10x more. It is a myth that the well-sorted work-life balance is fruitful only to the employee, it is also highly beneficial to the employers as well. Majorly because of the increased productivity of employees.

"Employers who are committed to providing environments that support work-life balance for their employees can save on costs, experience fewer cases of absenteeism, and enjoy a more loyal and productive workforce," said Chris Chancey, career expert.

One essential point to note when we talk about maintaining work and personal life is that, it isn't advisable to just divide the hours in a day, but to have the flexibility of working for long on one day, while you can take extra free time off on another day, the same week to compensate it. That flexibility to switch in between the work and personal life can simply be named as work-life balance.

Let's now discuss in detail on ways to create a better work-life balance, as well as how to be a supportive manager –

- **Accept that there is no perfect work-life balance** – When I continue speaking about work-life balance, I maybe am giving an ideal picture of you having a very productive day at work and returning back home early to spend the rest of your evening with your family and loved ones. But I certainly do not mean this, because it is close to being impossible in reality, while it looks just perfect ideally.

  Prioritizing your work and career while giving importance to practicing your hobbies and spending time with your family is the right kind of balance for any professional. Don't strive for the perfect schedule; strive for a realistic one. Balance is achieved over time, not each day.

  "It is important to remain fluid and constantly assess where you are [versus] your goals and priorities,"

  It is important to note that balancing feels different for different people, the procedures and planning that goes into finding the balance between prioritizing work and life. There are going to be hundreds of situations dropping by of health issues, continuous traveling, and loss of important people in your life, which will require yourself to be attentive towards your personal life too. Balancing it all, is the art.

  Balance is always achieved by consistent efforts and constant learnings from yours and other's mistakes over the period of time patiently. It takes a lot of frequent efforts, failures, and good company culture to achieve work-life balance.

  Some days you're attending to emergencies for your family, while on some days you're just stuck at work, but allowing yourself to remain open to redirecting and assessing your needs on any day is key in finding balance.

It is a prime and foremost thing to recognize that your progress shall never be compared to others' progress towards accepting that there's no perfect work-life balance.

- **Find a Job that interests you** – It is as simple as it sounds, a job that doesn't excite you to put up with your next day's tasks at work or if you're not looking forward any upcoming meetings or if you keep procrastinating your work because it doesn't interest you, then it's high time for you to realize that this position wasn't for you. There could be another candidate who could fill in your position happily while you can settle for the job that excites you.

When I proclaim this dissatisfaction of job, I do not mean that you have to love every aspect of your job, but you should be wise enough to know what the borderline of your tolerance level is.

Many corporate leaders recommend on taking up a job that you would've done it even for free. That's the kind of interest you need to develop while you're in an environment which demands for your productive attention and feasible time.

If your job is draining you, and you are finding it difficult to do the things you love outside of work, something is wrong. You may be working in a toxic environment, for a toxic person, or doing a job that you truly don't love. If this is the case, it is time to find a new job.

- **Prioritize your health** – As a leader, it is indefinite of you, if you're unaware that the healthy employees in your company are the roots of the tree that you'll be climbing on, while others stand there and appreciate you on your success. Your physical, mental, and emotional health should be one of the top priorities in your list of balancing your work and life.

Especially for women, this hits as hard as it can when they lose their focus over health and start prioritizing work. The importance of segregating and allocating time for practicing and inculcating habits healthier and the one that works best in both professional and personal life is priceless. Health is the primary concern when it comes to prioritizing in life. Maintaining the physical, mental and emotional health balance is the most difficult jobs one could do.

The taboos around addressing mental health issues are on the way to get destructed but aren't completely washed away. It's high time to consult a professional therapist if you feel like you needed to be heard and to voice your opinions. Talking your heart out without any barrier has been the most therapeutic care ever existed. Learn to adapt to it if necessary.

For some people in corporate, having a touch of any sport works like a charm, so being a leader, try and instill the feeling of bringing out the best sportsperson from every person. Arrange for weekend sessions post working hours or by taking few hours early off just so your employees can start off their weekends in a productive way and can carry that positive energy with them when they come back to work on a Monday morning.

The goal always has to be, to do less work, to be happier and productive when you're there. Educate your employees on the brighter side of having a regular practice of yoga, meditation and a quick short run. This quality in a leader, shows you genuinely care. And that's what matters.

- **Don't fear unplugging** – Unplugging doesn't always has to be cutting ties with the outside world and strictly avoiding work. It can also simply mean that you are taking a little time off from you work –related potential burnout and are practicing a small session away from professionalism on a daily repetitive basis.

When I talk about this, I mean one reading a book during their commute from home to work, rather than viewing your stacked up mails and piles of work that you'll be anyway stressing out for the rest of your day. Unplugging gives you a better clarity on how you want to invest your valuable time in making the rest of the time productive and worth spending.

The whole idea of this little unplugging everyday whilst doing your regular stuff, meets so many of the real-time expectations. It boosts your per day productivity ratio as an employee and also increases your company's performance as a whole.

A bigger picture painted works best always. Taking that time to unwind is critical to success and will help you feel more energized when you're on the clock. There has been a latest development of interest in listening to a podcast that's filled with experiences and life lessons. Other's experiences, quite often act better than all of the teachers.

Unplugging and unwinding has always proved that rewinding means to hit even harder and effectively.

- **Take Vacations** – As we discussed previously unplugging can be either a semi one or a prolonged vacation away from all work talks, scheduled lined up meetings, and dedicated working hours. Everyone deserves some time completely away from work as part of a vacation. Most employees are dumped with the thought of having piled up pending work when they return from a holiday. Do not fear away from enjoying yourselves thinking about the post-travel consequences.

The major motto behind the companies also offer you certain amount of permissible days off, is for you to come back with clearer head and calmer mindsets so you can enhance your potential and you can serve the company with the best of ideas you developed over the course of holiday.

It could be a weekday staycation somewhere away from the crowd of the city, or it could just be your solo trip to an island where unplugging is the best thing to be felt. Just you and your peace. According to the State of American Vacation 2018 study conducted by the U.S. Travel Association, 52% of employees reported having unused vacation days left over at the end of the year. The disruption of workflow, feeling left out after rejoining are a few of the major concerns that employees have addressed.

It is all about proper planning and the off season of your company when the burden upon everyone's shoulder is comparatively less. By planning properly you can make sure to reduce the extra responsibilities and burdens upon your team members. The truth is, there is no nobility in not taking well-deserved time away from work; the benefits of taking a day off far outweigh the downsides.

- **Allocate time for yourself and your close ones** – When we talk about an employee working in a corporate, it is pretty much evident to realize how messed up their work-life balance has been. One of the major things to do when we emphasize on balancing one's life is – to know how to allocate time for your loved ones and most importantly for yourself.

While acknowledging the fact that you have landed a good job, it is also important to recollect that you were also an individual with certain habits and aspirations in life, something that wasn't just work. Some employees are so lost in the process of developing their lives that they've forgotten how stress-less their lives have been before this.

Spending time with your loved ones, is one of the most helpful and therapeutic way of putting back your mental needs right in place. If one doesn't deliberately plan for setting personal life goals and attending to the needs of his family, spouse or children, he/she is bound to be living a partial life on its own.

No matter how hectic your schedule might be, you ultimately have control of your time and life. Creating a planner weekend dates with family or your spouse can help boost your private life immensely. It may sound absurd to put up a scheduled meeting date with the people you live every day, but it only helps your schedule be sorted and simplified. Spending quality time should be the priority. You may spend an entire day just wondering what to do for the rest of the day, and end up doing nothing productive, but that only tells you've not spent quality time.

Just because work keeps you busy doesn't mean you should neglect personal relationships. Also it is vital to remember that everyone is replaceable at work, and no matter how important you think your job is, the company will not miss a beat tomorrow if you are gone. This is a hard truth and we all learn it the hard way. The way your company celebrates your joy and supports you through your tough times can never equal the way your loved ones do.

So know when and how to prioritize your loved ones.

- **Set Boundaries and work hours** – Employee's physical and mental health burnout, has been a very common and frequent issue that has surfaced in most workplaces. It is quintessential to address the setting up of clearer boundaries after work and to have personal space when you're out of your workplace.

Know exactly when to stop worrying and thinking too much about work by setting strict shutdown at certain hour of the day. Try and manage to have a schedule strictly which enforces personal time away and weekends. The employees need to value the availability of flexibility in taking off from work once the work timings are up.

Even the colleagues that end up texting or calling you, needs to value and be sorry for disrupting your weekend or time-off for any reason. Learn to express and showcase your side of tranquility being disturbed. Feel free to them that your work hours have finished and that you shall get back, once they're working.

By doing this, your personal space is preserved and you have now successfully established a sense that you value your own personal time away from work. The next time they want to call you up, they'd rather have working hours in mind.

Whether you work away from home or at home, it is important to determine when you will work and when you will stop working; otherwise, you might find yourself answering work-related emails late at night, during vacations or on weekends off.

- **Learn to Set Goal and Prioritize** – When we talk about setting your goals of a day, a week, or even a year, it always means that you need to practice and stick to them as well. The practice of setting up work goals and to know how to prioritize the urgency of any work, will take you to places in corporate.

It's all about paying attention to little details about yourself. Know when you're the most productive and when your potential can be tapped to the fullest in a day and fit the most difficult ones from work into that schedule. This way you are meeting your goals effectively and effortlessly.

Prioritizing the 'need of the hour' works is a subtle art in itself. This helps you enhance your time-management strategies by analyzing your to-do list and cutting off time on those which require little to no time.

Avoid getting distracted by ignorable things like checking your phone every two minutes. This not only eats up your time, but also drags your energy levels to way low and shoots up your pessimism. More productive time at office means having the chance of starting early from work, which in turn means more time for self and/or family.

All this pro level of planning and preparing for setting up real-time goals doesn't come overnight, it's a process that needs to be acknowledged with patience.

- **Support the idea of 'Being a Supportive Manager'** – Flexibility is one of the most desired things for all the employees in corporate. Most employers have recently started to see the miracle of being flexible with their employees and in turn getting the best of outputs from them. However, they have made it a priority to grant employees access to a wider variety of benefits that fit their individual and family needs and that improve their health and well-being.

When we discuss the idea of being a supportive manager, I am advertising and marketing a notion of knowing and understanding your employees. Work-life balance can mean two different things for two differently distinct people. Some people view the idea of being 'A Supportive manager' as something that involves promotion, domination, unrealistic expectations and many more. This can all be proven wrong when understanding, friendliness and openness begins.

Being a strict manager can never make you a good and supportive manager. In our always-on world, balance is a very personal thing, and only you can decide the lifestyle that suits you best.

- **Know the craving of your Employees** – An honest and supportive manager will tell you that not everyone has a similar work-life balance. Because, we can never figure out what a person is handling in their lives. Some might be happy working remotely from home for a couple days a week. While some might see going to the office helps them function 10x better.

It always has been mere a personal choice. By 'Know your employees', I am asking you to address to the issues of employees personally. It's important to be open-minded and flexible.

- **Set a Good example** – This effect is as immediate as action and reaction. When you're working, you're imparting the idea of being able to inspire tens or hundreds under you. For example, if you being a manager send out a mail at 3 AM in the morning, then you're setting new standards for these employees to work just the same.

It is wise to realize that, working rightly and work hours can bring joy and calmness to your mind. Your employees will only look up to you, thinking I also want to be there someday, which again means that you're setting a great example for the ones under you.

- **Educate employees about their options** – Most of the times, for a corporate employee, it is not easy to manage personal and professional life simultaneously and gracefully. The struggle to have the employees know their multiple options being available is a generous and noble deal between an employee and employer. Sometimes making the couple of options available makes it a lot less heavy for the employee in picture.

Also, sit down with soon-to-be parents and discuss parental leave options. The struggle of new parents never goes unseen. Entire process of adapting to a whole new lifestyle with a new person and dealing with postpartum anxiety can be overwhelming.

This struggle applies to both new parents and newly-wed couples. Adjusting to a new environment is as challenging as it sounds. In situations like this, it is appreciated if you, as a leader showcase the options that are available extensively, like maternal/paternal leave, therapy sessions for employees, basically making them feel like a safe space to open-up.

CHAPTER 10

Life Is Too Short To Not Love What You Do For A Living

As far as we talk about equality at workplace, dignity and respect for work and equal treatment, it is all something that catches the attention of an employee in certain given time. But figuring out that your job doesn't give you a satisfactory sleep at night and makes your life uneasy comes the tougher way. Most of us don't even figure out that we are not enjoying the work and the perplexities drawn by a certain job that we are assigned. It is quintessential to behold that your job makes you want to thrive every single day of your life.

Most of us commit a common mistake by not choosing a career that we love as an important part of living a fulfilling life. And while a good salary and benefits may be high on everyone's wish list, many factors determine whether or not you'll cherish your job.

Why is being able to love what you do so important? While there are multiple factors revolving and deciding it, few of the notable ones are, being able to give your fullest to the company you're working for, when the company's principles align with that of yours, you can often leave the office feeling upbeat at the end of each workday when you love your job. While every day may not be amazing, a job you genuinely love will help you maintain a positive attitude on even the most challenging days.

If you are someone who hasn't analyzed if and why you love your job the most, then it's high time you do so. Some of the parameters you can use to rate your love for job are: Flexibility, Company culture, Great expectations, Fair pay, Goal-oriented leadership, Quality benefits, Room to grow, Challenging work, and most importantly work-life balance.

As the quote simply goes, "Life's short, make it worth-living". The truer essence of life and work together comes only when you crave for the stability that your company offers. According to a recent study, happiness does not directly correlate with money. It automatically ends once you start earning enough to feed yourself, have a shelter, and lead a decent respectful life. It also exclaims that happy people tend to earn higher salaries, and it stands to reason that these high earners are content – at least in part – because they have jobs they love.

For many, working at a job they love is more fulfilling, productive, and important than money. It can even lead to a higher level of success.

Enjoying your career is more important than earning a high salary or flashy title.

We are now going to dive into why it's important to feel passionate about your job and discuss reasons why people love their jobs so you can find a job you love too.

- **Feeling Fulfilled – *The best feeling your job can offer***

  Job fulfillment is defined as the level of contentment employees feel with their job. This goes beyond their daily duties to cover satisfaction with team members/managers, satisfaction with organizational policies, and the impact of their job on employees' personal lives.

  Your job definitely being a source of income shouldn't just override the fact that there's more to it. Once you taste the satisfaction of what you do for a living, there's no going back. If you don't enjoy what you do, you'll end up missing out on your life.

  Fulfillment deserves to be the focal point of living a balanced life. As we previously discussed, it is about how much motivated you are to wake up every day to go face your new work challenges. As long as you know your work will add up to only a minority of the overall stress you're facing, you are having a great job. Knowing that you have the flexibility of taking work from home if on some days you're unwell or have personal-life commitments, is an immense satisfactory deal.

Get to know about yourself. About what keeps you up, what makes you thrive and what pushes you to give your best? If you're a creative person you might not be happy in a conservative office environment. Visit the company's website and read their About Us page to get an idea of the values and general atmosphere you could expect.

Coworkers make a huge difference – A big part of loving a job is getting along with your coworkers. Feeling compatible with the office team will make you feel like a valued member of the company. Check out the social media posts of the company to get an idea of employee outings or volunteer activities that give an indication of employee personalities. These things add up to the pile of satisfactory criterions.

- **Being Passionately Productive** – Passion for work simply means you feel excited about what you do. You find meaning and purpose in your work. You tackle each day with focus, never making excuses for why you can't get things done.

"Passion is energy. Feel the power that comes from focusing on what excites you." - Oprah Winfrey

Productivity follows the trail of passion and progress. It often tends to talk about the way you do, when you do, what you love doing. A person tends to be excited about work, if they feel drawn towards the work. They'll know that they're going to learn well when they're given challenging situations.

There are multiple ways to engage yourself in productivity and increase passion for work – few of them are – Shift your perspective, Match work to your goals, Connect with others, Do more of what you love, Embrace growth, Take a break, Consider a career change and many more.

It is important to feel motivated and inspired in whatever you're doing. Without the urge to excel in your performance, your progress will tend to remain stagnant. Productivity allows you to become more efficient, which makes room for downtime and encourages work-life balance.

Being passionate about work not only sets you right on the path, but also helps you get through the grind throughout the day. It also pushes you to take that extra mile to understand and process the new concepts at work. It simply creates enough engagement between you and your company.

- **Inspiring Others** – You start inspiring others when you eventually start doing something that's out of the course of what most people assume to be the right way to do it. The risk that surrounds the decision of taking an abnormal path, is although huge but becomes satisfactory is important.

  Think about what you would tell to your friend or colleague when they wanted to choose their job satisfaction over stability. If you feel you'll ask them to stick on to the feeling of achieving job fulfillment, then you are definitely inspiring them to be a better employee. When you do take that leap yourself, you become an inspiration to others.

  Personally speaking, as a mother myself, I find it hard to manage having a life where I can give importance to my work while I also make my children happy. There have been times when I had to choose between my personal life details and professional emergencies. I try to balance it quite well. I personally hope my kids grow up to see how important working was for me, how I have gracefully managed it, and for them to get inspired to choose a career that makes them reach high.

- **Success Follows – *when you do what you love***

  It is often said that we work productively and efficiently when we do what we love. Your job, it doesn't feel like something you're merely doing just for earning a living, when you're enjoying the whole process by indulging in it completely and wholly.

  It makes it easier to get through the trials and tribulations of business ownerships. It helps you focus largely on benefitting the company while you focus on your own interests. You wouldn't do your job because you're compelled to do so, taking orders from your superiors wouldn't seem troubling because you'll be focusing on doing something that excites you.

The main reason to do what you love is your happiness. Finding that place doesn't only provide contentment, but makes you more motivated and better equipped to do the best job possible. You won't just be happier – you'll be more productive.

The working instinct you develop will not be bound to anything other than the drive you acquire. It comes very natural and effortless. The challenges put forth you, will be something that you're ready to explore and not something that burns your energy. You want to be where you're challenging yourself.

The biggest realization one has when they're in a place where they love their job is that, you see yourself as the only and true competitor. You come to terms that you should out-do your previous performance every time.

This kind of a corporate attitude gets developed when you're chasing stability, consistency and love for your work. And when you chase these qualities, success starts chasing you.

Now, after discussing why is it quintessential to know if you love your work and why it is so important to do so, we need to discuss what factors pushed you into becoming an image you made of yourself as a child. Ask these 4 questions to yourself to be better and determine your next step –

- **What did you want to be as a Child?**

  While it might sound absurd to go back to your childhood days of admiration of future, when ambitions and goals changed every day, it is essential to find and filter out the common base in all those. Not everyone would have wanted to become an engineer, working extra-time sacrificing a work-life balance. Some would've wanted to grow up and become a businessman. You need to figure out the story behind the things that made you happy.

  It sure has to come from 'Somewhere'. That somewhere could be watching your grandparents talking about politics and justice, it would've instilled a sense that when you grow up, you want to be just and fair to people around you. Some cases when you grew up with a dream of becoming a teacher, would be insisting that you will grow up to become a person who likes imparting knowledge and being around kids.

Always try to bridge your career goals with what you thought you'd become when you call yourself grownup. *Because there always is a bridge.*

The basic motive should be that you do what you love to do. Because that would keep the child inside you curious and sane.

- **What would your Family/Friends Identify as your Strengths?**

In most cases, we fail to mirror our strengths and weaknesses in all terms. We get carried away with the daily struggles of life and forget to stop for a while and think about how and where we are lacking professionally. It is utmost important to realize and encounter the strengths that got concealed while you were paving a way for your success.

It is sometimes very common that our family/friends know us better when it comes to recollecting our lost/forgotten aptitudes. Also sometimes it becomes crucial to gather different perspectives just so you can look for yourself and dig more from your strengths.

Some days, it is quintessential to see that our family is our biggest support system and our functioning starts depending in these factors. When it technically shouldn't happen, it exists considering we're interdependent beings. We believe accepting the validation and peacefulness from the ones we look up to. Let us normalize family having our back.

Keeping up with the constantly varying modifications and expectations by the corporate standards makes it hard for the employees to act even close to being ideal. Choose your job in a way that aligns with your goals, strengths and capabilities. Being stuck at a work that you don't enjoy doing will not serve you with any good.

What you consider your strengths may differ from your family and friends' perceptions. *So always remember to take advices and perspectives from people around you, but follow only those that you deem right for yourself.*

- **Who was your biggest role model growing up?**

This simply talks about how much influence a role model has on growing minds. Remember when our parents just kept talking about freedom fighters, good politicians, and revolutionary beings from history? That somehow definitely impacted our childhood thought process. A child that has no role models has not grown up to become something great in life. At the same time, when a kid looks up at someone and learns, he/she learns better.

Did you love this person because they helped people? Did they have special skills that you desired? Did you find similarities between their and your abilities? By thinking about why you looked up to this person, you might find a job that would suit you. And I cannot stress on how important it is to love what you do, and do what you love.

Sometimes it might look futile as your childhood goals, inspirations and ideals would seem completely different. But the task is to actually find something that's common from the very base and foundation. Because it is proven that we love/ hate a person for several unknown reasons as well.

- **What did you truly dislike doing?**

While it is quintessential to remotely notice and follow any leads on what your strengths are, it is also advisable to keep your weaknesses on check. It can be dreadful if you're doing something you're not good at, or something that doesn't push you to take that extra mile happily at work.

Understanding what you dread doing can be as powerful as having perspectives in shaping your career path in the right direction. If you don't take this into account, you may find yourself back at square one and looking for another new career down the road.

Determining what you want to do next involves a bit of searching. Consider your strengths and weaknesses while deciding your next move, and even try venturing back to your roots to find the next course of action.

As we talk about finding a job that loves you, and something that you love, the thing about getting paid right valuably is necessitated as well. You need to find a right balance between the deserving pay and desired working space. For example, if you hate working with long tables of data in spreadsheets, a career dealing with extensive amounts of data may not be the right move for you.

Individuals differ in their interests, strengths and perceptions. Einstein said, "Every person is a genius. But if you judge a fish by its ability to fly high, it will give its entire life believing that it is an inane".

To have a meaningful work life, it is essential that individuals align work with their interests and strengths. This will ensure that the passion toward work is maintained and you look forward to doing your job well everyday.

Special Heartfelt Thanks

There's not an ending without remembering and thanking the ones who mean everything to me. My mom who is the pillar for my success and her continuous support and belief in me helped me to realize successful mothers are not the ones that never struggle, but they are the ones that never give up despite the struggles. **Thank you for being my leader, protector, encourager and a friend!** For me no influence is as powerful as that of my mother's!

My father is the role model I looked up. He always helps other people and always tries to do the right thing no matter what is the cost to himself. "Dear dad no matter where I go in life you will always be my number one man." One of the key things I learned from my father is **"First deserve then desire."** We must first develop the capability before we start demanding something. My dad's courage and leadership qualities will remain greatest inspiration in my life.

Special Thank you to my great companion, life partner, Mr Sushant Gaonkar for believing in me and supporting me through the ups and downs of my life. His values have been constant source of inspiration for me and who always encourages me to make an impact on society through my work. **Thank you for being my rock!**

My two children, Trishul and Taniya, who have pushed me to be better, stronger, kinder and more patient. They have helped my voice become stronger. **You both are the greatest gifts life has ever offered me!**

Thank you all my readers. You have chosen this book because you have burning desire and are aspiring to become leaders!

If your actions inspire others to dream more, learn more, do more and become more... then you are a leader!

\- **Spoorti Nayak**

Connect With Author

If you want to continue to learn and connect with author and be part of 'VOICE OF A WOMAN LEADER', please send an email to **spoorti.nayak@gmail.com**.

You can also follow her on:

LinkedIn - https://www.linkedin.com/in/spoorti-nayak

"Wishing you all a flourishing and successful career ahead by instilling **INTEGRITY, INSIGHT AND INCLUSIVENESS."**

Milton Keynes UK
Ingram Content Group UK Ltd.
UKHW021521130324
439151UK00007BA/117